THE CATHOLIC GENTLEMAN

SAM GUZMAN

The Catholic Gentleman

~

LIVING AUTHENTIC
MANHOOD TODAY

Foreword by Dale Ahlquist

IGNATIUS PRESS   SAN FRANCISCO

Cover photograph by Mary Grace Pingoy
Cover design by John Herreid

© 2019 by Ignatius Press, San Francisco
All rights reserved
ISBN 978-1-62164-068-4 (PB)
ISBN 978-1-68149-649-8 (eBook)
Library of Congress Control Number 2018931251
Printed in the United States of America ∞

*To the Immaculate Virgin
and to my wife and children*

CONTENTS

Appendices

FOREWORD

The word *gentleman* has fallen into disrepute, along with the word *man*. There is a connection. Gentlemen have become ungentlemanly in direct correlation with men becoming unmanly. It started, however, with gentlemen not doing their bit.

It is a paradox that the word *gentleman* was traditionally applied to a man not immediately associated with gentleness, as it were. It was a word given to a knight. Knights were dubbed "Sir" when they had achieved a certain valor, proving themselves brave and worthy in every respect, and often that involved bravery in battle and actions that were anything but gentle. Along with his title, a knight was given property. He was the defender not only of a fortress but also of a field. And a family.

The knight knew how to plant and build as well as how to fight. He also knew how to entertain, to put on a feast, to sing, and to recite poetry. And he knew how to pray. He always set an example—when he stood, when he walked, when he sat, when he talked, and when he knelt, before his lady, and before his God.

Putting on armor was a rare event but a necessary one. The knight's greatest strength was in his restraint. He won love and respect without having to brandish his power. He followed an established set of rules.

He knew that freedom existed within those rules—
freedom for himself and for everyone who depended
on him. He was civilized; he was not a barbarian. He
was gentle because he was polite. G. K. Chesterton
points out the forgotten connection between the words
polite and *police*. Both refer to self-restraint, to keeping
order, to following rules. Politeness watches over the
polis, the city.

Along with politeness, which is about keeping order, the other characteristic of a gentleman is courtesy,
which, as Chesterton says, means courtly behavior,
the way a person acts in the presence of royalty. To
show courtesy, as a gentleman would do, means to treat
every man as if he were a king and every woman as
if she were a queen. Courtesy is sublime humility and
charity. As Chesterton notes, Saint Francis of Assisi
treated even animals with courtesy.

Politeness and courtesy both rely on self-restraint.
But, as Chesterton also points out, men have that
"strength in reserve" that is sometimes called laziness.
Yes, the virtue of self-restraint, like every good thing,
can be put to the wrong use, as other virtues can be
corrupted into vices; and a common male weakness,
laziness, is the tendency to let other people do things.
But the gentleman does things for himself. It is why
he is a leader and an example. And it is why, when
gentlemen started taking advantage of their position, it
sparked a bad reaction from women. The male privi-
lege to lead (which is to serve) became the opportunity to take and to abuse, to indulge and simply to have

one's way. Gentlemen lost their sense of responsibility, their sense of honor, and their sense of reality.

When men stopped behaving like gentlemen, women stopped behaving like ladies. Women started asserting their rights because men had stopped recognizing them. Women started doing manly chores because men had stopped doing them. Women became detached from the home because men had become detached from the home.

The corruption of knighthood led to the rise of feminism. When gentlemen started caring only about the power and prestige that came with their position, they stopped being gentlemen. And the men who followed their example stopped being men, stopped acting responsibly and started acting selfishly, stopped leading with politeness and started leading with power. They cast aside their self-restraint and started strutting their mere strength. They became warlike, not in noble acts of defense, but in dastardly acts of aggression. Feminists merely followed the same bad example. With no gentlemen around to treat them like ladies, they stopped acting like ladies and instead started imitating all the worst unrestrained male behaviors. Ladies quit being queens when gentlemen quit showing courtesy.

Men have stopped showing courtesy. One of the most obvious places we see a lack of courtesy is on the Internet, in the unrestrained manner in which people address each other. The virtual world is not a virtuous world, as people type things to their onscreen adversaries that they would never say to a person sitting across the table. At least, not yet: There is nothing to stop this behavior from carrying over into the real world.

Not only are men not behaving like gentlemen on the Internet; they are not treating women like ladies. A man who regards a woman as no more than a soulless erotic image existing only for his gratification has become a barbarian, the very thing the good and gentle knight had to fight against. We need to bring back these knights. We need to bring back true gentlemen.

Sam Guzman has given us something we desperately need: a valuable, readable book to help make young men into gentlemen.

—Dale Ahlquist

PREFACE

Solomon, the wise king of old, opined somewhat bitterly that of the making of books "there is no end" (Eccles 12:12). And even though he lived three thousand years before mass-market paperbacks, e-readers, and Amazon existed, he was right. New books are published every day—hundreds, perhaps thousands, of them. As you glance at this book, you may be wondering: Why should I read this one?

That is a fair question, and there's only one legitimate answer: This book offers you something—some truth, some insight, that will leave you a better, happier, more complete man.

Now, some men write books because they are truly wise and have profound insights to offer. But I'm just an ordinary husband and father. I wrote this book not because *I* have some unique wisdom to share but because I believe that the Catholic and apostolic Church does.

I've found through experience that the Catholic faith is not some dusty museum piece of a religion, fit only for grandmothers and starry-eyed fanatics. Though it has been handed down through twenty-one centuries, it is not some petrified relic. It has outlived wars and persecutions, despots and diseases, and countless dangers, both internal and external. It has transformed sinners into saints and has sustained countless men just like you, who are struggling through this pilgrimage we call life.

I've found that, beneath all the caricatures and criticisms of the Catholic Church, she possesses something both relevant and real—the faith that is "ever ancient and ever new".[1] I firmly believe that this faith has something to say to you as a man living today, and what it has to offer can change your life. For the substance of the faith is not some ivory-tower abstraction, or lifeless doctrines in heavy theology textbooks, but, rather, an encounter with a living Person, Jesus Christ. And he alone can make you the man you want and need to be.

Perhaps you're skeptical. Maybe this sounds like so many pious platitudes. Or maybe you're all in and can't wait to get started. Either way, I invite you on this journey of Catholic manhood. It is a path of adventure and struggle, failure and triumph, battle and romance. It isn't an easy road, but it is the only one worth taking —because the destination is so much better than you can imagine.

This book is intended to guide you toward that destination. It is not an exhaustive treatment of every aspect of manhood, past and present, nor is it an in-depth theological treatment of what it means to be a man. Others have already done an excellent job of writing books like those (see *Behold the Man* by Deacon Harold Burke-Sivers, for one example). Rather, this book offers short chapters on various aspects of manhood.

[1] Saint Augustine, *Confessions* 10, 27.

Designed to be read in just a few minutes, they stand alone, focusing on a single idea. I pray that, like a good compass, each chapter is a reference that points you to what matters.

Let's go.

I

The Quest for Authenticity

Authentic. Genuine. Handcrafted. Vintage. *Real.*
Something about those words stirs something
in a man's soul. We don't like fake. We like things
that are solid, strong, and can stand the test of time.

Case in point: Ever since I was a little kid, I've had a
fascination with old cars. My stepfather would take us
kids to classic car shows, the kind in oily McDonald's
parking lots with French fries plastered to the pavement and the Beach Boys blaring over loudspeakers.
Vintage hot rods and muscle cars would line the parking lot in row after row of ferocious beauty.

These cars were enough to make a Prius-driving,
granola-eating eco-warrior screech in terror. Massive,
eight-liter engines throbbed, pulsed, and growled, emit-
ting bass notes so guttural you could feel them pound-
ing in your chest. Oversized superchargers whined and
howled, sucking air into jittering, four-barrel carbu-
retors. Dancing side pipes belched exhaust, and tires
melted in plumes of acrid smoke as drivers dropped
the clutch, unleashing hundreds of horsepower on the
quivering pavement.

It was awesome.

I still love muscle cars. Mustangs, Chargers, Challengers, Road Runners—you name it. Those names get my blood pumping.

But do you know what I love about those old cars? It's more than the beefy engines and the loud exhaust systems. I love that they are real—all steel and rubber and gasoline. There's no plastic made to look like chrome; no garish façades; no synthetic quarter panels; no fake air intakes; no tricks, no deceptions. What you see is what you get.

Sure, today's sports cars are faster, with better quarter-mile times and more efficient engines. But there's something magical about those old powerhouses, something that can't be replaced by touchscreen navigation systems, torque-vectoring differentials, or EPA-mandated fuel-efficiency ratings. Muscle cars represent a time when steel was really steel, not a cheap imitation—before everything was tamed and neutered by excessive government regulations. Just watch the car-chase scene from the movie *Bullitt*, and you'll see what I mean.

This book isn't about cars. It's about men. But I think there's an important parallel. For decades, modern men have been fed a steady diet of fake—and, deep down, we hate it. From a very young age, we've been taught, explicitly or implicitly, that the purpose of life is to accumulate as many mass-produced commodities as possible, starting with a big house in the suburbs with a huge TV in the living room and a late-model SUV in the driveway. We are told we *need* Internet-connected refrigerators, voice-controlled home automation systems, and the latest smartphones and tablets. And none of these mass-produced commodities is real. Imitation leather, artificial flavoring, plastic, particleboard—all fake, disposable, and replaceable. I recently saw an imitation-stone façade being glued on the front of a house under construction. Ridiculous.

The whole world is just a grand illusion, it seems, with nearly everything made to look, feel, and taste like something it isn't. It's all so many lies, the exact opposite of the straightforward honesty of those old cars.

So, what do many men do? They rebel.

Those bearded hipsters with tattooed arms and lumberjack shirts—they're rejecting something. They're saying no thanks to the vanilla suburbia of their parents and the hollow McMansions with professionally manicured lawns and oversized SUVs. They're turning their backs on the cult of fake.

What do they choose instead? Anything authentic, artisan, local, and small batch. Anything that tells a story, that involves a craft or smacks of "old-world" traditions. They live in big industrial lofts in refitted factories, and they frequent antique shops. They ride bikes and read old books. They support small, local business. And not a few have been known to smoke pipes and buy typewriters.

I am not suggesting that becoming a hipster is the answer. The hipster's quest for authenticity can often be taken to an absurd extreme. It is hard not to chuckle at a suspendered, handlebar-mustachioed young man riding a penny-farthing down a crowded city street. Reactionary movements have a way of getting out of hand rather quickly. It is also true that vintage trappings and tattoos can be artificial substitutes in their own right —a shallow veneer covering an infantile attitude. Yet the fact remains that, however misguided, these trends indicate a hunger for something of substance. They point to a discontent with the cheap commercialism and artificial façades of suburbia.

The hipsters of Brooklyn and Portland aren't the only ones rejecting fake and mass-produced commodities. Not everyone will pursue this quest for the authentic in the same way. Some become bikers, or punks, or vegans. There are nearly as many subcultures as there are people. But the point remains: Men, especially young men, crave the authentic, the tested, the proven and reject the artificial, mass-produced alternatives.

The question is: How do we know if *we* are the real deal?

Blessing of an Automobile or Other Vehicle

The Church seems to have a blessing for everything, and that includes your car. Whether you have a 1968 Charger or something as mundane as a minivan sitting in your driveway, here's a blessing for your priest to pray over it:

℣. Our help is in the name of the Lord
℟. Who has made heaven and earth
℣. The Lord be with you.
℟. And with your spirit.

Lend a willing ear, Lord God, to our prayers, and bless this vehicle with your holy right hand. Direct your holy angels to accompany it, that they may free those who ride in it from all dangers, and always guard them. And just as, by your deacon Philip, you gave faith and grace to the man of Ethiopia as he sat in his chariot reading the Sacred Word, so, point out to your servants the way of salvation. Grant that, aided by your grace, and with their hearts set on good works, they may, after all the joys and sorrows of this journey through life, merit to receive eternal joys, through Christ our Lord. Amen.[1]

---

[1] "Blessings of Things Designated for Ordinary Use", *Rituale Romanum*, no. 15, posted on Sancta Missa, https://www.sanctamissa.org/en/resources/books-1962/rituale-romanum/54-blessings-of-things-designated-for-ordinary-use.html.

2

The Gift of Manhood

M EN REJECT THE INAUTHENTIC, but we also fear it. We fear it because we're worried we might *be* it. No man wants to be a sham, a phony, or a fraud. In other words, we want to be *real* men. We want to know that we are the genuine article. We want to know that when we act tough or courageous or confident, it isn't fake. We don't want to be hollow men wearing a mask of manhood that covers our insecurity. Much of our maturation is merely the quest to prove, to ourselves and to others, that we are real, authentic men. There is one small problem: There is no one to tell us when we have reached the goal.

No one becomes a man alone. No matter how hard we try, we can never make men of ourselves. Manhood is always something that is received and bestowed on us by the wider collective of men. And until someone tells us authoritatively, "You are a man, my son!" we may question and be dogged by a nagging doubt. We may never really be sure if we are the genuine article rather than a mere imposter.

Almost all traditional cultures had distinct initiation rituals for young men, often in the form of a painful trial or challenge, such as extended fasting, survival alone with no tools, long periods of solitude, or close brushes with death. Although these rites of initiation were intentionally difficult, even dangerous, they proved without question, both to the boy and to the other men in the community, that the aspirant had passed the test. There would be no room for doubt: The boy had become a man.

Some initiation rites are downright horrific. The Sateré-Mawé people of Brazil famously use bullet ants to initiate their young men as warriors. If you've never run into a bullet ant, count yourself fortunate. Its sting is considered the most painful insect bite on earth. Each sting offers the equivalent pain of being shot with a bullet (thus the name), with the intense agony lasting twenty-four hours. But the pain isn't the end of the sufferings—a single sting can also cause nausea, paralysis, hallucinations, vomiting, and cardiac dysrhythmia. The terrifying part is, the Sateré-Mawé don't use just one ant in their initiation rite.[1] They use about thirty.

A glove is woven out of leaves, and the sedated ants are placed in the lining with their stingers directed at the wearer. As the ants regain consciousness, they struggle to break free from the glove's lining, becoming increasingly desperate and angry. It is then that the boy must insert his hand into the glove and endure the wrath of thirty bullet ants for approximately ten minutes, dancing and chanting to cope with the pain.

[1] "Sateré-Mawé Initiation", *Cultures and Customs*, November 13, 2016, https://sites.psu.edu/mgeitnerrcl/tag/satere-mawe/.

One ritual isn't enough, either. This agonizing ceremony must be done twenty times before a young boy is considered both a man and a warrior. And you thought confirmation class was painful.

Gruesome initiation rites may seem bizarre and even sadistic to us. Yet think about these rituals from a young boy's perspective. No matter how horrific the test he has to face, once it is over, he no longer has any doubt that he is a man, nor does his community. He has proven that he has what it takes, and no one can take away that achievement. Whenever he hears the whisper of doubt about the authenticity of his manhood, he need only remember that he passed the test.

The Sateré-Mawé are not unique. There are other such rituals of initiation into the warrior class, such as the grueling boot camp for aspiring Navy SEALs known infamously as Hell Week. All cultures, traditional or modern, understand that the more an aspiring warrior can prove he can endure physical and psychological suffering, the more equipped he will be to protect others from harm.

The story is told of a young man who called his father to complain about the rigors of his military training. His father listened patiently but had little sympathy for his son's suffering.

"Is anyone trying to kill you?" he asked.

"Well, no," replied the son.

"Exactly. They are trying to prepare you to face those who will be."

3

Fathers and Sons

M UCH OF THE CRISIS of modern manhood is due to
the absence not only of initiation rites but also
of initiators. According to the United States Census
Bureau, only 23.5 percent of American homes have stable families with both a mother and a father.[1] Approximately twenty million children in the United States
are living in fatherless homes.[2]

This lack of male involvement in the raising of children, especially sons, has been devastating. Sociological
research has found that fatherlessness affects all aspects
of a child's development, including physical and emotional health, educational achievement, and economic
status.[3]

While it is easy to blame the sexual revolution of
the 1960s for the epidemic of fatherlessness, there is
more to the picture. In his book on manhood, *Iron
John*, Robert Bly makes the case that the real crisis of

---

[1] Vicky Waltz, "Raising Boys without Men", *BU Today*, January 17,
2007, http://www.bu.edu/today/2007/raising-boys-without-men/.
[2] "Fatherless Epidemic", National Center for Fathering, http://fathe
rs.com/wp39/wp-content/uploads/2015/07/fatherlessInfographic.pdf.
[3] Ibid.

fatherhood can be traced back to the Industrial Revolution—the explosion of mechanized technology in the late nineteenth century that completely transformed the dynamics of the home. Commenting on this transformation of the family, Bly notes:

> The traditional way of raising sons, which lasted for thousands and thousands of years, amounted to fathers and sons living in close—murderously close—proximity, while the father taught the son a trade: perhaps farming or carpentry or blacksmithing or tailoring. . . . The love unit most damaged by the Industrial Revolution has been the father-son bond. . . . The Industrial Revolution, in its need for office and factory workers, pulled fathers away from their sons, and moreover, placed the sons in compulsory schools where the teachers are mostly women.[4]

The Industrial Revolution largely removed fathers from the home, leaving young boys to be raised by their mothers and, increasingly, female teachers, who inevitably sought to tame their maleness. No longer could fathers intensively instruct their sons in the art of manhood, either by word or by example, being largely absent except for a few hours in the evening.

This absence of the father in the home is problematic, as fathers have historically been the ones to instruct their boys in socially needed and accepted behavior and to initiate them into the class of men. Especially in Western society, the father was responsible for both

[4] Robert Bly, *Iron John: A Book about Men* (New York: Vintage Books, 1992), p. 19.

modeling masculinity and then announcing to his son that he had passed from boyhood to manhood. The absence of a father in the home has meant no instruction, no initiation, and this lack has produced several generations of "lost boys" who don't know for sure if they can wear the badge of manhood with pride, or if they are destined to be mere children forever.

With fathers absent, the burden of initiation has fallen to father figures who test and prove us, albeit unofficially—perhaps a drill sergeant or a football coach or a business mentor who drives us to perform. Whoever it is, he must be someone who can test us, set the standard of achievement, and eventually welcome us to the world of men. But sadly, many men lack even a father figure.

Without clear role models and proper instruction in the art of manhood, countless men today have stumbled into adulthood unsure about what manhood really consists of and with no understanding of what separates a man from a boy. Thus, many thirty-something men are living very much like overgrown teenagers for whom manhood is an ideal they have no idea how to attain.

Add to that the current confusion over whether maleness even exists as a sexual reality, rather than a socially constructed gender one can choose as he will; school bias against boys; and the falling number of men attending college, and you have the makings of a full-blown crisis of the meaning of masculinity.

It's easy to point out the problems plaguing modern

manhood. I could go on for many more pages. But all these various problems point to a larger issue—the loss of masculine identity. We don't know how to be men because we don't even know what a man is anymore. Before we can dream of being gentlemen, we've got to understand what a man is, and how to be one.

4

Putting the Man in Gentleman

I AM IN THE MARKETING BUSINESS, and one of the fundamental facts of marketing (and life in general) is that context gives meaning. How a product is framed has everything to do with how people will perceive it and how much they will want it.

Take, for example, Marlboro cigarettes, the best-selling cigarette brand in the world. Marlboros first appeared in England in the 1870s, where they were marketed as a cigarette for women. They were entirely unsuccessful. Undeterred, the owners of the Marlboro brand decided to sell them in America, again targeting women. The messaging was designed to attract delicate, refined sensibilities, so it was emphasized that Marlboro was a "mild" cigarette suitable for polite company. Once again, the cigarettes were a failure, and they were pulled off the market around the start of World War II.

The brand was revived in the 1950s, right around the time the health risks of cigarettes were first being publicized, and was again marketed to women. This time the selling point was the new filter, which would provide a safer smoke. Once again, sales were poor.

Then everything changed. The marketing team decided to scrap the female-oriented messaging and reinvent the Marlboro completely as a cigarette for men. They launched a series of ads featuring rugged, enigmatic cowboys. The first ad featured a cowboy sporting a tattoo, squinting at the camera with a look that would make Clint Eastwood proud. The cowboy image launched Marlboro into decades of unparalleled success. The product was the same, but the context changed the meaning, for what a thing means is as important as what it is.

What does *man* mean? The great crisis of the modern world is not one of theology, or a lack thereof, but, rather, one of anthropology—of what it means to be human.

The key to understanding something is to learn its purpose. What was it made *for*? Think of a hammer in a toolbox. To an alien, it might seem a strange composite of rubber, steel, and wood. It has an odd shape. It's heavy and a bit unwieldy. What is it for? Maybe it is a ceremonial object, or perhaps an eating utensil. It might seem very mysterious to someone who knows nothing about it.

But to us, a hammer makes sense because we know it is used to drive nails. We know its purpose and see it in its wider context, so it makes sense to us.

But what is the purpose of a man? What is he made for? What is the wider context that defines masculinity? To understand that, we must first understand what it means to be human.

First and foremost, human beings were made for communion, for relationship. Our lives make no sense apart from others. No one spontaneously springs to life from an empty void. Each of us originated from the union of our mother and our father, and our bodies formed and developed in our mothers' bodies. We were born into a community, in relationship with others from the first moment of our existence.

That is not to say that these initial relationships are always ideal. All too frequently, children are born into tragic circumstances, received with malice or neglect. But although these relationships with uncaring parents may be fractured, they are still relationships.

Of course, we can intentionally or unintentionally isolate ourselves from others. Some hearty souls have been known to flee all human companionship, such as Chris McCandless, the young man who abandoned his family and lived in an abandoned bus in the Alaskan wilderness. Yet this severing of all communication must still be a conscious choice, and even when it does occur, it is rarely healthy—mentally, spiritually, or physically. Many who have sought to escape human contact have ended up going mad. This is why solitary confinement is such a devastating punishment. McCandless died of starvation because he was cut off from human contact.

Furthermore, our bodily maleness reveals the fact that we were designed as incomplete in and of ourselves. Male biology needs female biology to make sense, so relationships are inscribed in the very makeup of our anatomy. We are one half of an equation, one piece of a bigger puzzle.

Our lives don't make sense outside the context of relationships. Even Adam, before Eve came along, had a Father—God himself—to whom he was related and owed his origin.

This others-oriented view of man flies in the face of the individualism our society encourages. According to the modern way of thinking, individuality is the greatest good. Radical autonomy should be pursued at all costs. In fact, we are told we can create our own reality. According to Supreme Court Justice Anthony Kennedy, "At the heart of liberty is the right to define one's own concept of existence, of meaning, of the universe, and of the mystery of human life."[1]

One has a right to define his own concept of existence? That's clearly absurd to anyone with an ounce of common sense. You can try to define your own concept of existence, but it won't change reality. And if your concept of existence does not correspond to reality, you will simply be living a delusion. There are hospitals for people who live like that.

Like it or not, we were made to be in relationship. We are not autonomous agents independent of others. As the poet John Donne famously said, "No man is an island."

Still, it is clear that men and women relate differently. So what makes a man unique? There are many facets

[1] Planned Parenthood v. Casey, 505 U.S. 833 (1992).

of men's uniqueness, but I want to examine just one: Men are unique in that they *generate*. They bring forth the raw, unformed materials that are then refined and shaped by women. They plant the seeds that women nurture.

A simple example is a traditional farming couple of the past. The husband would rise early and hitch the horses to a plow and, for hours on end, perform the backbreaking labor of clearing, plowing, and planting the fields. At harvest time, he would sweat under the hot sun, collecting the fruits of his labors.

Yet, as important and difficult as planting and harvesting are, a bushel of wheat is still a long way from a loaf of bread. When the husband would bring home the harvest, it was up to the wife to make something useful out of it. She would grind the grain into flour and make it into bread for the family to eat. The husband generated the raw materials, and the wife made something beautiful and nutritious out of them. This is one reason such work is called home*making*. It is considered an art requiring great skill for a woman to take the raw materials of life, generated and produced by her husband, and make something wonderful out of them.

The same principle can be seen in the generation of human life. In the sexual act, men "plant" the seed, but it is up to the woman to nurture it and form it over nine months into a beautiful little person. Men generate the raw materials, while women fruitfully receive and nurture them. Both roles are essential to mankind's well-being.

That is not to say that men cannot bake a loaf of bread, or that women cannot plant or tend a garden or a field; nor does it mean that men cannot help nurture children or that women cannot have a job. Nevertheless, it is true as a general principle that men tend toward wild, raw, and unrefined *generation*, and women tend toward nurture, care, and formation, bringing order out of chaos. A good mother will balance, but not eliminate, the wilder impulses of her sons, teaching them manners and refinement. In a similar way, a good wife will make fruitful the raw materials her husband produces, whether it be in the formation of a new human life or in beautifying her house and making it a home.

Fatherhood and paternity mean generation, and ultimately, our ability as men to generate reflects the Fatherhood of God, for whom "all paternity in heaven and earth is named" (Eph 3:15, Douay-Rheims).

5

The Many Faces of Manhood

W HO WAS MORE OF A REAL MAN: General George Patton or Mister Rogers? Based on a particular set of gender stereotypes, many would say that Mister Rogers wasn't nearly as manly as "Blood and Guts" Patton. But I disagree.

At first glance, General Patton had all the attributes we often associate with manly men. He was aggressive, tough, fearless, and foul-mouthed. He walked with a swagger and acted with bravado. And it's true—he was a great man, as learned as he was relentless on the battlefield.

Mister Rogers, on the other hand, was soft-spoken, gentle, and had a natural affinity for children. He sang songs he invented and wore sweaters his mother made. He talked about feelings, and he prioritized relationships.

The truth is, both Mister Rogers and General Patton were *real* men, just as the crusader Saint Louis of France and the gentle, nature-loving poet Saint Francis of Assisi were real men and real saints. Manhood has many faces, and we would be foolish to reduce masculinity to only one archetype. To do so would create a caricature of masculinity.

Great men throughout history have lived their masculinity in many ways. Some, like Rembrandt and Shakespeare, are artists and poets who are sensitive to beauty and emotion that others miss. They communicate the wonder of life and the human experience, and we are the richer for it. Others, like Saint Thomas Aquinas and Albert Einstein, are scholars who shed light on man's deepest questions and the mysteries of the universe. Others, like Fred Rogers and Saint Giuseppe Moscati, are relational or physical healers who restore what is wounded. Still others, like General Patton or King John Sobieski of Poland, are warriors who defend what is just and good and true.

That is not to say that manhood is a subjective reality, or to deny that men have certain predominant traits. There *are* traits that are prominently masculine, such as a desire to fight for and defend the good and the vulnerable, an attraction to risk and danger, and a desire to leave the safety of home and explore the unknown. Yet not all men incarnate these traits in the same way. Some satisfy their desire for conflict and conquest on a chess board, while others satisfy it in a boxing ring. Some enjoy exploring the wilderness and hunting wild beasts, while others get a thrill out of conquering difficult intellectual problems and illuminating unknown realms of thought.

It would be absurd to claim that Michelangelo was less of a man because he (probably) couldn't bench three times his body weight. It would be ridiculous to claim that Mozart wasn't truly masculine because he composed orchestral music instead of heavy metal. It would be undeniably wrong to claim that Tolkien was less of a man because he wrote stories instead of practicing martial arts. Men are men, but not all men are the same.

God has given us men unique talents and abilities, and we shouldn't suppress them in some misguided quest to make ourselves into Arnold Schwarzenegger's Terminator. Raw aggression is not the only legitimate expression of manhood. Of course, acknowledging this truth is not an excuse to grow flabby, weak, and undeveloped. Whatever our gifts, we are called to develop them to the glory of God and strive to be the best we can be. Whether we are publishers or pugilists, we must live with the same virtue and integrity. We must develop an *inner* strength, no matter how large our biceps happen to be.

In addition, whether we are scholars or athletes, it is healthy to develop areas that are outside our natural inclinations. It is praiseworthy for the bookworm to develop his physical abilities, just as it is good for a professional soldier to develop a taste for reading. Although it isn't strictly necessary to our masculine vocation, we should nevertheless strive to be well-rounded men, even if it takes us outside our comfort zones. Doing so will enable us to grow stronger both inwardly and outwardly.

Manhood is not a monolithic thing—it has many

faces. Not all men look the same, and this is by God's design. We should never scorn others for not being exactly like us. Nor should we insist that all men look the same, conforming to an arbitrarily chosen archetype— unless, of course, that archetype is Jesus Christ. For he alone shows us what completely integrated masculinity looks like.

And yet, even in our imitation of Christ, we will discover a startling paradox—the more we become like him, the more we become fully ourselves. The more fully Christ lives in us, the more fully we will discover our uniqueness. Our talents and gifts will shine forth the clearer and we will understand, perhaps for the first time, the truths that there are many gifts, but one Spirit, and we, though different members, are one body in Christ (see 1 Cor 12:4, 12).

6

Style Advice from a Saint

RECENTLY, WHILE SHOPPING FOR GROCERIES, I saw some-one shuffling down the aisle in pajama pants and slippers. Her hair was dirty and unkempt, and it looked as if she had just rolled out of bed. The worst part was, she seemed oblivious that there was anything inappropriate about frequenting a public place in such a state.

We are a long way from the days when men would always wear a hat, jacket, and tie outside the house. Photos of old baseball games show men in the bleachers in coats and ties—in the hot sun, no less. There were certain social expectations about how one was to dress in public. It wasn't just stuffiness: Being well groomed and caring for one's appearance was deemed a matter of respect for others. Slovenliness was considered unthinkable to anyone who had an ounce of dignity and self-respect.

But that was then. Now we live in a world where anything goes. Aside from public nakedness, there are essentially no fashion taboos left. In such a climate, it is worth asking: How should a Catholic gentleman dress? I can think of no better way to answer that question than to quote a saint—a saint who happens to be a Doctor of the Church. I'm referring to Saint Francis de Sales. In his famous work *Introduction to the Devout Life*, de Sales gives timeless advice on how we should care for our appearance. Here's what he says (slightly edited to remove advice specific to women):

> St. Paul expresses his desire that all Christian women should wear "modest apparel, with shamefacedness and sobriety" (1 Tim 2:9)—and for that matter he certainly meant that men should do so likewise. Now, modesty in dress and its appearances depends upon the quality, the fashion and the cleanliness thereof. As to cleanliness, that should be uniform, and we should never, if possible, let any part of our dress be soiled or stained. External seemliness is a sort of indication of inward good order, and God requires those who minister at His Altar, or minister in holy things, to be attentive in respect of personal cleanliness.
>
> As to the quality and fashion of clothes, modesty in these points must depend upon various circumstances, age, season, condition, the society we move in, and the special occasion. Most people dress better on a high festival than at other times; in Lent, or other penitential seasons, they lay aside all gay apparel; at a wedding they wear wedding garments, at a funeral, mourning garb; and at a king's court the dress which would be unsuitable at home is suitable. . . .
>
> Always be neat, do not ever permit any disorder or untidiness about you. There is a certain disrespect to those with whom you mix in slovenly dress; but at the same time avoid all vanity, peculiarity, and fancifulness. As far as may be, keep to what is simple and unpre-

tending—such dress is the best adornment of beauty and the best excuse for ugliness.

St. Peter bids women not to be over particular in dressing their hair. Everyone despises a man as effeminate who lowers himself by such things, and we count a vain woman as wanting in modesty, or at all events what she has becomes smothered among her trinkets and furbelows. They say that they mean no harm, but I should reply that the devil will contrive to get some harm out of it all.

For my own part I should like my devout man or woman to be the best dressed person in the company, but the least fine or splendid, and adorned, as St. Peter says, with "the ornament of a meek and quiet spirit" (1 Pet 3:4). St. Louis said that the right thing is for every one to dress according to his position, so that good and sensible people should not be able to say they are over-dressed, or younger gayer ones that they are under-dressed. But if these last are not satisfied with what is modest and seemly, they must be content with the approbation of the elders.[1]

There you have it. Fashion advice from a Doctor of the Church. His rules are simple and timeless. First, be modest. Modesty is often associated with coverage of skin, but this is not really what it means. At bottom, it means humility; it means not drawing excessive attention to yourself. Second, be aware of your context and dress appropriately for it. Don't wear flip-flops and a

---

[1] Francis de Sales, *Introduction to the Devout Life*, pt. 3, chap. 25, posted on Catholic Treasury, http://www.catholictreasury.info/books/devout _life/dev69.php.

tank top to a funeral. Third, be neat and clean; attend to basic grooming. It's a sign of respect for others to care for your appearance. Fourth, don't be overly fussy about your appearance—don't be a dandy or a fop. Manicures and eyebrow waxes are not becoming.

As Catholic gentlemen, we should always dress with dignity and respect for ourselves and others. We should shun slovenliness. But we also shouldn't be overly fussy about our appearance. We should be simple, unaffected, classy, and elegant. If we follow these wise, practical rules, we will be, as Saint Francis puts it, "the best dressed person in the company".

7

Virtue

O N JUNE 6, 1944, the largest seaborne invasion in history commenced. More than 160,000 Allied troops sailed from England on approximately 5,000 ships. They arrived at the coast of Normandy, France, early in the morning. A cold wind was blowing, and the skies were gray with thick clouds. The icy waters were choppy, and waves tossed the small amphibious landing craft that carried troops toward the shore. Some men became sick from the rocking of the waves and strained nerves.

Young men, many no older than eighteen, smoked cigarettes with shaky hands as they prepared to meet their fate. Huge shells, fired from battleships, shrieked overhead before crashing into the coastline, leaving behind craters several yards deep. The order was given to disembark. The ramps of the landing craft dropped, and icy waves rushed in. The young men plunged into the frigid waters of the English Channel, holding their rifles high over their heads. They were greeted by an onslaught of enemy machine-gun fire bursting from heavily fortified concrete bunkers. Many were torn to pieces before they could take a single step. The water ran thick with blood and body parts. And yet the men kept coming.

As a young boy of twelve, I visited the beaches of Normandy. I saw the massive pockmarks from the brutal shelling that shook the earth, craters so large you could run down inside them. I climbed down into the concrete nests that housed the machine guns, their walls still scarred from the Allied gunfire. I gazed on the perfect lines of pale white crosses lining the cemeteries. There, I learned something about virtue.

Young men, most only a few years older than I was at the time, fought and died on that coast. They were probably scared to death, watching their friends get blown to bits, not knowing whether they themselves would live or die from one moment to the next. But they didn't flee. They performed their duty. They fought when everything in them was telling them to run away. They persevered and pressed on when they could have turned tail and run for cover. They endured a hail of merciless bullets because it was the right thing to do. These young men weren't perfect, but they had more fortitude, more courage, than most, and they fought for justice.

What made these men? Virtue. Virtue is what makes a man. It's what made those men plunge into icy waters and fight and keep fighting for an idea, a principle —freedom.

And what is virtue? Virtue is a habit or disposition of doing what is good in every circumstance, even the most difficult. More precisely, as the *Catechism of the*

Catholic Church tells us: "Human virtues are firm attitudes, stable dispositions, habitual perfections of intellect and will that govern our actions, order our passions, and guide our conduct according to reason and faith. They make possible ease, self-mastery, and joy in leading a morally good life. The virtuous man is he who freely practices the good" (1804). In other words, virtue is the habit of doing the right thing, at the right time, for the right reasons.

Interestingly, modern neuroscience has discovered something scientists call neuroplasticity. This means that the mind is not static but, rather, grows and develops over time, adapting itself to repeated actions. It's much like a muscle. If you exercise parts of your brain over time, they will grow stronger. If you check your phone first thing every day, your brain will adapt to this choice. It will become easier to check your phone and harder not to. It will become a habit.

The discovery of neuroplasticity confirms what philosophers and theologians have known for centuries—that repeated choices become habits, and these habits make us who we are. If we repeatedly do the right thing, it will become easier for us to do the right thing. And the easier choosing the good becomes, the harder it will be to do the *wrong* thing. The whole trajectory of our life will incline toward what is right.

Virtue is critical to a happy life because it makes us truly free, not a slave to the impulse of the moment. Virtue is peak performance of all our abilities. A virtuous man functions at his highest, in the way he was meant to function. He is a man of integrity, in the sense that he is *integrated*. His mind, body, and soul fit together in an integrated whole.

A man without virtue, on the other hand, is helpless. He is led by his appetites, his passions, which scream at him all day long. He has no ability to control himself, to say no to his whims and impulses. He is controlled by them, swept along like a dead fish in a current. Men without virtue are the whiners who quit when the going gets tough. They are overgrown boys who shrink in fear at the slightest challenge. These are the men who retreat to "safe spaces" in order to recover from the trauma of hearing the opinions of those who disagree with them.

On the level of nature, virtue consists of four things: prudence, justice, fortitude, and temperance.

Prudence is the ability to make wise judgments, to see all the factors and make the best choices. This ability doesn't come automatically. Left to ourselves, we are impulsive. Children are a perfect example of this. They have hardly any ability to say no to themselves except through fear of some consequence. Even then, it is difficult. They see a piece of candy and they eat it, whether or not it will ruin their appetite for dinner.

The adult, the man, however, is prudent. He can see where things are going. He knows that if he eats all the candy in the bag he will get a stomachache and, more than likely, a cavity. So he resists. With time and practice, he develops prudence. When faced with decisions far more consequential than eating a piece of candy, he learns to understand the consequences of actions and behaves accordingly. He can sacrifice the pleasure of the moment for a greater good; he can put off what he wants now for what he wants more.

Prudence, too, keeps the other virtues in check. A thirst for justice, unchecked by prudence, can easily turn into vigilantism or revenge. This is why prudence is known as the charioteer of the virtues. It guides the others as a horseman guides a team of horses or a steering wheel steers the power of an engine.

Justice is the firm resolve to give to God and neighbor what is owed to each. It is giving others their due, and it is the most social of all the virtues. Often, this virtue is seen only in a negative light, in the sense of just punishment for wrongdoing. Yet, justice isn't merely negative. It is a positive acknowledgment of something. The president of a country, whether you like him or not, is owed a certain level of respect because of his office. Justice gives that respect, even in spite of disagreement. Moreover, it respects the rights of others. It sees in each person a dignity that should not be violated and accordingly treats the person with honor. Justice, then, governs the relationships between all people. It ultimately leads toward the common good and the flourishing of society.

Fortitude is stick-to-it-iveness. It is a dogged determination in the pursuit of the good, even when it would be much easier to quit. Fortitude is courage in doing what is right. When everything was screaming in those GIs at Normandy to flee in terror, fortitude is what kept them fighting.

We all face trials in life. Sickness, loss of loved ones, trouble at work, failures, and flat tires. In the face of these obstacles, fortitude will keep us pressing forward. Like all virtues, it is developed with time and repeated effort. The first time we face our fears, look obstacles square in the face, and "saddle up anyway", to quote John Wayne, it feels almost impossible. But the next time it's a little easier, and the time after that it's even easier, until eventually, we develop a habit of fortitude.

Temperance is moderation in all things. It is the ability to avoid excess and extremes, even extremes in the other virtues. It keeps us from going off the deep end as we are often prone to do.

Temperance is especially important when it comes to our appetites. Eating two pizzas by oneself and finishing them off with a whole tub of ice cream is not temperate. A beer or two is moderate. A shot of tequila in honor of each year since your birth is not. Temperance helps us moderate our desires and keep them in check. It helps us find the healthy mean that lets us enjoy pleasures without becoming sick or ending up with a headache or worse.

Children are controlled by their feelings and appetites. The mark of maturity, on the other hand, is the ability to keep one's desires in check, to guide them as a rudder guides a ship. Virtue is the habit of doing the right thing. We are not born virtuous, therefore acquiring virtue takes effort and practice. The exertion is worth it, however, because virtue is the sure way to happiness.

8

A Brief Guide to Happy Drinking

I GREW UP PROTESTANT, and in the Baptist churches my family frequented when I was young, alcohol was strictly prohibited. It wasn't simply frowned upon as unhealthy; rather, it was condemned as downright immoral. I even heard pastors go to great lengths in their sermons to explain that the wine Jesus made at the wedding at Cana and the wine he drank at the Last Supper wasn't really wine at all, but grape juice. When we did receive communion—usually once a month at an evening service, when fewer people were there—we received Welch's grape juice in a tiny plastic cup. Just as Jesus did, right? Wrong!

As Catholics, we don't believe alcohol is immoral, and, in fact, monks have a long tradition of brewing beer of extremely high quality (and alcohol content). Even Saint Paul admonishes Timothy to drink wine for its medicinal purposes (1 Tim 5:23), and the psalmist declares in a hymn of praise that God created wine "to gladden the heart of man" (Ps 104:15). Benjamin Franklin's quip about God creating beer because he loves us and wants us to be happy has scriptural support!

Despite the claims of Baptist preachers, Christ certainly did create more than a hundred gallons of wine at the wedding at Cana, and it was wine of very high quality. Catholics are not puritans, and if we look at both Scripture and tradition honestly, it is impossible to argue that alcohol is intrinsically immoral. It is a gift from God to be enjoyed responsibly.

What *is* immoral, however, is abusing alcohol. One of the essential human faculties that separates us from the beasts is our rationality—our ability to deliberate, to make moral choices, and to be consciously aware of ourselves, of others, and of our Creator. Drunkenness surrenders these faculties, handing over the control of our reason and will to the influence of alcohol. And as the tragedies of domestic abuse and drunk-driving-related deaths demonstrate, surrendering these faculties is not simply wrong but can be downright deadly.

How, then, are we to drink *virtuously*? How can we enjoy alcohol without surrendering to drunkenness? Here are a few simple guidelines.

First, drink in moderation. This should go without saying, but when it comes to alcohol, it can be very easy to overdo it. We may begin with good intentions, but before we know it, we have had a few drinks too many. There is no defined amount that constitutes excess. Tolerances differ: One person may be able to drink all night and maintain perfect control, while another may feel buzzed after a single glass of whiskey. We all know our own limits, so it is wise to set a reasonable limit for ourselves. If three beers are too much for you, stop at one or two. If you start feeling tipsy after five shots of whiskey, stop at three. Be moderate, and you will enjoy drinking to a greater degree. The people around you will enjoy your company more too.

Second, never—and I mean *never*—drink because you are unhappy. G. K. Chesterton, as usual, offers some sage advice here:

> Drink because you are happy, but never because you are miserable. Never drink when you are wretched without it, or you will be like the grey-faced gin-drinker in the slum; but drink when you would be happy without it, and you will be like the laughing peasant of Italy. Never drink because you need it, for this is rational drinking, and the way to death and hell. But drink because you do not need it, for this is irrational drinking, and the ancient health of the world.[1]

Drinking to drown your sorrows is the surest way to abuse alcohol and to hurt yourself and others. Drink only to enhance your happiness, and your drinking will be sane and healthy.

Finally, drink for conviviality. *Conviviality* is a word we don't use enough these days. It simply means the joy of being together. There are few things more joyful than the buzz of warm conversation among friends around a bright bonfire on a summer's evening, enhanced by a glass of scotch and a cigar. Properly used, a good drink can loosen us up and free us from our anxious self-consciousness. Instead of nervously wor-

[1] G. K. Chesterton, *Heretics*, The Collected Works of G. K. Chesterton 1 (San Francisco: Ignatius Press, 1986), p. 92.

rying about what others might think—a sure way to stifle any conversation—a pint of beer can set us free to enjoy one another's company.

Drinking well can be a joy. Drinking carelessly can, without exaggeration, ruin your life. Let temperance always be your rule. I will conclude with a toast from Pope Benedict XVI, a true German who knows how to enjoy a good drink: "We are on the Lord's team, therefore we're on the winning side. . . . Let us raise our glasses."[2]

[2] Quoted in Paul A. Zalonski, "Pope Lunches with Friends, Speaks of Struggle against Evil", *Communio* (blog), May 22, 2012, http://comm unio.stblogs.org/index.php/2012/05/pope-lunches-with-friends-spea/.

9

Fatherhood

M OMENTS AFTER MY FIRSTBORN SON, Peter, was born, he was placed in my arms—a tiny, frail helpless bundle. He was surprisingly alert. Unlike many newborns, he was calm and was not crying. His eyes were wide with wonder as he gazed curiously at my face. I felt as though my heart would burst. This tiny life would be molded and shaped by mine. I would always be his father, and he would always be my son. The weight of that realization was dizzying in its enormity.

About two years later, Peter, now a chubby toddler, ambled up to my side and took my face in his hands as I bent over. "Daddy," he said in his lisping voice, "you are my daddy."

"Yes, Peter," I responded, "and you are my son."

You are my son. My beloved son.

In those words, we find the key to all successful fatherhood. I always thought that being a good father was a matter of experience, or even more naïvely, book learning. If only I knew all the right things, I would do all the right things. And yet, the more I learn about fatherhood through both failure and success, the more

I realize that being a good father flows inevitably from having first learned to be a good son.

Much of who we become as men is shaped by our experience of sonship. Our masculine identity is wrapped up in the words "You are my beloved son." Likewise, much of our woundedness and insecurity as men flows from our relationship with our fathers—specifically, from those moments when our identity as sons is obscured by our fathers' sins and failings. Even the best earthly fathers are less than perfect, and they can leave scars that affect not only who we become as men, but also how we as fathers relate to our own children.

At the heart of the father-son relationship is reciprocal love. The identity of the father is to will what is good for the son; the identity of the son is to receive the father's love and return it in trustful surrender and obedience. When the son is convinced that his father desires and wills what is good for him, he can safely place himself, with complete vulnerability and without fear, in the arms of his father.

This relationship of selfless giving and trustful receiving finds its primordial model in the relationship of the Holy Trinity. God the Father gives and begets, from all eternity. He exists for the Son. The Son, in turn, receives the love of the Father in trustful abandonment and obedience. He exists *from* the Father. The Holy Spirit is the personification of the love shared by the Father and the Son. The Spirit exists *with* the Father and the Son.

Although the model is clear, the reality in a fallen world can be quite different. Because of Original Sin, we are all caught in a very sticky web of brokenness and sin. Every person enters this world bearing the wounds of the failings and the sins of others and, in turn, inflicts wounds of his own.

Earthly fathers, no matter how good and well intentioned, do not always will the good for their children. In fact, even the best fathers can break their sons' trust. Failed promises, uncalled-for anger, inattention, selfishness—fathers are prone to all these things, and they can have lasting effects on children. To varying degrees, fathers can say in so many words, "You are not my beloved son. You are a son of whom I am ashamed. I wish you were anyone but who you are. Do what I want, or I will reject you. My love is conditional, and you must measure up." These often-unspoken communications, intentional or not, can leave us with deep-rooted wounds of shame and insecurity and with feelings of inadequacy. They damage our ability to receive love. They close our hearts, and we become guarded and distrustful, skeptical and cynical. We learn to fear instead of to trust.

As adults, we can look back at our childhood and perhaps see the ways in which our fathers failed us and shaped who we are. Perhaps we were never told, "You are my beloved son." Perhaps to this day we have a deep insecurity because our fathers never affirmed our identity. Forgiveness is necessary. Then again, perhaps our identity *was* made clear to us, and it has made us whole.

If we are to be good fathers, and on a more basic level, complete men, we must find or rediscover our masculine identity as sons. No matter how good or poor our earthly fathers were, no matter what wounds of the heart we bear, we have a heavenly Father who will never fail us. Whether we realize it or not, each of us is a son, adopted by the eternal God and bought with a price.

"God sent forth his Son", teaches Saint Paul, "born of woman, born under the law, to redeem those who were under the law, so that we might receive adoption as sons" (Gal 4:4–5). Saint John, too, proclaims in wonder: "See what love the Father has given us, that we should be called children of God; and so we are" (1 Jn 3:1).

We do not ponder this mystery nearly enough, but if we did, it would bring us great healing. God loves you as a cherished child. He takes your face in his hands, looks you in the eye, and says, "You are my beloved son, in whom I am well pleased." And that identity will never change. It can never be taken away.

Your ability to be a father is rooted in your identity as a son. You cannot be a good father until you are first a beloved son. Know this: You are a son of God. He loves you and has bought you at great cost to himself. Ponder this mystery. Let this identity seep into your bones, into the core of who you are. Receive his love, and abandon yourself to his goodness. He will never fail you.

How to Bless Your Children

A forgotten ritual you can revive in your home is the blessing of your children. This can be done each night before bed, once a week on Sunday, or whenever you want. To bless your child, trace the sign of the cross on his forehead (I dip my thumb in holy water first, but this isn't necessary), and say the following: "May almighty God, Father, Son, and Holy Spirit, bless you, my child, for time and eternity, and may this blessing remain forever with you. Amen."

That's it! It's very simple, and if you do it frequently, your children will come to love and expect this simple practice.

10

The Code

M Y WIFE AND I ARE FANS of *Star Trek*, the famous sci-
fi series created by Gene Roddenberry. There's
something stirring about exploring the vast reaches
of the galaxy with nothing but a trusty ship, a sea-
soned crew, and your wits. The philosophical themes
explored along the way make it even more satisfying.
Ah, the final frontier.

Of the various starship captains featured in *Star Trek*,
my favorite is Jean-Luc Picard. Picard is bold, com-
manding, and decisive. He is a quick-witted and bril-
liant strategist. There are few alien species that can out-
think him. He loves music, literature, and archaeology.
He is a truly cultured gentleman—not to mention that
he possesses the stentorian voice of a Shakespearean
actor.

But the most important of Picard's traits, I believe,
is that he lives by a strict code of ethics that guides his
every decision. He is as principled as they come, willing to sacrifice comfort and convenience to a higher
law.

His internal code is demonstrated in many episodes,
such as in "Chain of Command, Part 2", in which he is

taken captive by a ruthless Cardassian enemy, Madred, who wants nothing more than to break Picard's will. He begins to torture Picard, humiliating him by stripping him naked and hanging him by his arms all night. The next day, Madred tells Picard that a small torture device has been implanted under his skin that can inflict extreme pain at Madred's command. He demonstrates it on the lowest setting, and Picard falls to his knees in agony.

Behind Madred's head shines a bank of four lights. To end the torture, Picard must do one thing: Say there are five lights. It is so utterly simple, so temptingly easy: Simply say there are five lights, even though there are only four.[1]

Repeatedly, Picard is asked to say it. Repeatedly, he refuses to lie, defiantly shouting, "There are four lights!" Each time, his commitment to reality is greeted by new doses of extreme pain. Truth comes at a cost, yet he refuses to bend, to deny what is real. His inner commitment to the truth, to reality, is more important to him than ending the suffering. He has a backbone, an internal strength that helps him resist the distortion of reality that is being forced upon him.

If there is one thing we can say about modern men, it is that we do *not* live by a code. Few, if any, of us would endure brutal torture if we could end it merely by saying there were five lights when there were really four. Modern men are frequently pragmatists. We do

---

[1] The scenes in this episode are borrowed from George Orwell's famous novel *1984*.

what is convenient and comfortable in the moment, whatever causes the least pain. Our culture encourages this kind of practical, path-of-least-resistance thinking. We puzzle over men who would suffer torture for *anything*. We wonder at the firebrands of the past who would go to war at a moment's notice to defend some principle they believed in. Are there *any* principles we believe in strongly enough to suffer for them? It's hard to say.

Yet, every authentic man lives by a code. Unprincipled pragmatism is inconsistent with authentic manhood. Mature men do not make difficult decisions based on whims, convenience, emotions, or whatever happens to be the least painful. No, they rely on objective principles, on truth and justice, to choose the right thing to do.

But for a code of life to exist, a man must acknowledge a higher law, an objective truth to which he pledges allegiance. No one will endure prolonged suffering for muddle-headed, convoluted, or contradictory ideas. No one will be tortured for vague, feel-good notions such as tolerance or sexual license. The idea is absurd. To live by a code, one must believe in unchanging principles that aren't mere feelings or opinions but are true at the deepest level.

Sociologists speak of two kinds of values: *intrinsic* and *extrinsic*. Intrinsic values motivate us to do things when we know we will get nothing in return. We do these things because they are the right things to do or because we find joy in doing them. We do them as ends in themselves. Such things include playing with our children, praying, and heroic actions such as rushing into a burning building to save a life. Extrinsic values, on the other hand, motivate us to do things to win the approval of others—such things as working hard to get a promotion, working out to impress women with our physique, or perhaps buying an expensive new car as a status symbol. If we are to be men of integrity, we must be motivated first and foremost by intrinsic values. We must do the right things for the right reasons; we must have the priorities of Christ and his kingdom.

The martyrs went joyfully to unspeakable torments because they were convinced that Christ is real, that the Resurrection is real, and that heaven is real. That truth was worth suffering for. All they had to do to avoid their brutal fate was offer a pinch of incense to Caesar. It was so simple, so easy. But they wouldn't do it.

They couldn't face the Coliseum full of lions ready to tear them to pieces unless they were convinced of a higher reality—not just intellectually, but in their heart of hearts. They believed that the God they had come to know was worth suffering and dying for. They weren't afraid of anything that anyone could do to their bodies.

The question we must ask ourselves is: What do we believe deeply enough to die for? Until we can answer that question, we cannot know what we are living for. What are the truths at the deepest level of our being that guide our choices and our conduct? What compass guides us; which star is our true north? What are the intrinsic values that motivate us?

The world daily offers a thousand temptations. They are little compromises, small betrayals. Just offer a pinch of incense to a false god. Just say there are five lights when there are really four. But though these compromises seem harmless, they can be our undoing—the ruin of our souls and our humanity.

11

The Body

S CIENTISTS COME UP WITH SOME ODD IDEAS. Perhaps being unusually smart makes them liable to think
up rather silly things. Take, for example, futurist Ray
Kurzweil's idea that the human brain could be down-
loaded into a computer. According to Kurzweil, the
human brain functions like a computer, and therefore,
it shouldn't be too hard in the near future to plug us
in and download all our memories, and even our per-
sonalities, into a machine.

To those who want to live forever without God, this
sounds appealing. After all, we wouldn't be limited by
these clumsy bodies that are prone to disease and pain.
Unfettered from the mortal coil and armed with the
power of supercomputer processors, our intelligence
could roam free for all eternity, in uncompromised
bliss.

Perhaps to a scientist, this sounds wonderful. I, for
one, do *not* relish the idea of living in circuits for all
eternity. Regardless, the real problem is that our brains
don't work like computers at all.[1] The more neurolo-

[1] Robert Epstein, "The Empty Brain", *Aeon*, May 18, 2016, https://a
eon.co/essays/your-brain-does-not-process-information-and-it-is-not-a
-computer.

gists learn about the brain, the more they realize that the mechanistic, computer-based metaphor for the brain doesn't hold true. There are no hard drives in the brain, no processors, and no circuits like those of computers. Our memories and experiences simply aren't packaged neatly into little libraries that can be identified and reproduced elsewhere. Memory and cognition involve the whole brain and even the body. A person's experiences, even from before birth, change the structure of his brain. Each experience makes his brain more and more distinctive, more and more unique and unrepeatable. That is why none of us experiences the same event in the same way. Each sees things according to the totality of his experiences.

Put another way, certain memories are not stored in only one part of the brain—the whole brain stores memories, and it changes with each new experience in a way we do not understand. That is why, despite the vast sums of money spent to map it, scientists have yet to unlock the "code" of the brain that would make a computer transfer possible. Our minds are not machines or glorified computers. They are much more mysterious than that.

Why does all this matter? It matters because for centuries, even millennia, man has been tempted to separate the mind and spirit from the body. We tend to dislike our bodies, frail and corruptible as they are. They age and decay, while our minds may still be quick and active. Our bodies seem so limited, while our spiritual and mental powers strain toward infinity.

The most infamous of all the heresies related to the

mind-body divide is Gnosticism. The ancient Gnostics viewed the body, and all created matter, as evil. According to them, the spiritually enlightened person would seek to transcend the universe of created things, as no good could come of it, and live a life of pure spirit. Through the centuries, other heresies have cropped up, borrowing from Gnostic dualism to varying degrees. And the Church has fought all of them, for the Church knows that God made the body and the world, and he made them very good.

In a way, all of us moderns are Gnostics to a certain extent. Society places a great emphasis on education and the cultivation of the mind while disparaging trades and jobs that require physical labor. Technology, too, has exacerbated the mind-body divide in the modern world. We once lived in an agrarian world, in which most men and women labored physically every day out of sheer necessity. But since the earthquake of industrialism shook the world, fewer and fewer of us do any bodily work.

I sit at a computer all day, working with my mind for hours. At times, my back aches and my legs grow stiff. I understand why some might see the body as a hindrance.

A prosperous technological society will eventually begin to neglect the body as ease increases. Yet it is critical to remember that we are not pure spirits. We are not souls that happen to have a body; we are souls that are, in a sense, inseparable from our bodies. Our bodies are tremendously important, for they reveal spiritual realities. "The body, and it alone," says Saint John Paul II, "is capable of making visible what is invisible: the spiritual and the divine."[2] As Christians, we believe that our souls live on after our bodies die, yet this is only a temporary state, for we will later be united with our glorified bodies for all eternity. Heaven isn't liberation from the body. It's merely a new way of living in the body.

We do not need to be liberated from the dead weight of our bodies. To think so is a grave mistake. We are not persons trapped in a body. Our body is the physical manifestation of our soul, and not a mere machine to house an intrinsically superior intelligence.

Should we ever doubt that the body is good, we should remember that God himself has a body and will have it for all eternity. Jesus Christ, the Eternal Brightness of the Father, the Logos, deigned to take on a frail human body. He knew what it meant to sweat, to bleed, to ache, to grow weary. He felt, he tasted, he suffered, he enjoyed and savored. He felt the breeze in his face and the nails tearing his flesh. He is the God-Man, God with a human body that still bears the scars of his wounds. Let that sink in, for a more tremendous mystery than the Incarnation cannot be found. We could ponder it for all eternity, and most certainly will.

---

[2] John Paul II, general audience "Man Enters the World as a Subject of Truth and Love" (February 20, 1980), http://w2.vatican.va/content/john-paul-ii/en/audiences/1980/documents/hf_jp-ii_aud_19800220.html.

As Catholic men, we must reject notions of mind-body separation and learn to cultivate an appreciation for our bodies, caring for them and recognizing their intrinsic dignity. Our bodies are not to be despised or abused, while we venerate our intellect and our spiritual capacity. It is true, our bodies will rot and return to dust. But they will also be raised again in glory and will be part of us for all eternity.

12

Tradition

O NE OF THE MOST PREVALENT MODERN MYTHS is that of radical autonomy and individuality—that is, that we enter the world as if it were a reality to be bent to our will; that we have complete control of our own destiny and identity. According to this worldview, we need nothing and no one. I, in the words of the poet, am "the captain of my soul".[1]

The myth of autonomy says that the world is a blank slate, empty of any true meaning or content except that which we give it. There is no objective reality, only the reality that exists in our heads, and the world changes based on our unbridled passions and subjective inclinations. The world becomes but a grand projection of the self. When we encounter those inconvenient obstacles known as other individuals, we are compelled to bend them to our internal reality, often by force or violence.

At radical odds with the idea of autonomy and self-assertion is the idea that tradition is at the heart of reality—tradition not in the sense of mere archaic ceremony or custom, but in the sense that reality is a gift

[1] William Ernest Henley, "Invictus".

to be received. The simple fact is that we are born into a world, and into a community of persons, that preceded us and that the world and the community shape us more than we shape them.

Almost everything we are is determined without our consent, and even before we can consent. We do not choose our parents or our name, or our place of origin, or our hair or skin color. We don't even have any say over our personality and tastes, which are influenced by our genes. Much of who we become as adults is a product of circumstances beyond our control, and the choices of others affect us nearly as much as the choices we make for ourselves. We do not merely create who we are; we also receive it.

Those who have embraced the myth of autonomy are struggling against reality as it is. They are fighting a losing battle against the truth. As a result, radical individualists despise tradition. They reject it and want to smash anything that smacks of it, as they would smash the bars of a prison. If a man really believes the world is what he makes it, he must reject anything that even resembles a received reality, anything that reminds him of what has come before him in the long chain of existence—whether it be liturgical, architectural, or social.

As men seeking to be Catholic gentlemen, we must reject the modern lie of autonomy and embrace the giftedness of things with wonder and gratitude. Masculine identity, like the Catholic faith itself, is a gift, a *traditioned* thing. We do not make manhood in our own image. We do not decide what it is. Manhood is something that preceded us, a reality that we must strive to achieve and receive, not remake according to passing fads or allegedly progressive thinking.

Likewise, the Catholic gentleman should not reject religious tradition but, rather, should treat it with respect and reverence. The Catholic faith is universal, in that it is for all times and places. In the strict sense, there is no such thing as modern Catholicism or medieval Catholicism or primitive Catholicism. It is all a unified reality, and religious tradition acknowledges this fact in its language, its ceremony, and the content of its faith. Yes, progression and change can and do occur, but such change should be organic, like the growth of a body. The faith, both doctrinally and liturgically (these two aspects are inseparable), is handed on and is not to be re-created according to our tastes or cultural trends.

A Catholic gentleman should be immediately suspicious of anyone, layman or cleric, who is eager to do away with tradition, which is the living memory of the Church. Such a desire and disdain communicates a wish to remake the faith in one's own image; to impose cultural or personal whims on the faith, rather than humbly receiving it as it is.

A Catholic gentleman is a man of tradition. Rather than arrogantly struggling to bend and shape reality according to his egotistical desires, he receives what has been preserved and handed on by others. He loves truth, the reality of things as they are. Rather than seeing himself as a radically autonomous agent, he acknowledges that he is but one link in a great chain of existence that came before him and will continue after him. He therefore strives to become worthy to preserve and pass on what he has received to future generations.

13

Suffering

WHEN I JOINED the wrestling team in high school, I was as wimpy as could be. Perhaps *wimpy* isn't a strong enough word. I was pathetic. I was a five-foot-tall, ninety-pound, asthmatic weakling. The only things I conquered were stacks of books.

For most of my life, I had been plagued by severe asthma and allergies, and as a result, I was sheltered from doing anything difficult or physically strenuous, for fear I might end up in the emergency room. And that was fine by me—more time to read.

But when I got to high school, something in me snapped. I was tired of being a pushover. I wanted to struggle. I wanted to overcome. I wanted to do something that pushed me to the limit. I may have been scrawny, but I had a fighter's soul.

The problem was, I was too small for football and too short for basketball. I wasn't coordinated enough for baseball or anything else. Wrestling, though, had weight classes, which was great for someone my size. How hard could it be? So wrestling it was.

But boy, was I in for a shock! Having never done anything physically tough in my life, I simply wasn't ready for the difficulty of wrestling. The English language is hardly adequate to describe my suffering during those two to three hours of practice. It was agony beyond all reckoning. Stairs, sprints, push-ups, and wall sits—until my vision blurred and I puked my guts out. My muscles quivered and burned, my lungs strained for air. The pain seemed as though it would never end, and I hated every minute of it.

And then came the wrestling matches themselves. I was tossed around like a rag doll. The world turned crazily in all directions as I was pinned in positions I never thought possible. I felt powerless as opponents slammed me into the mat to the cheers of their fans. It was humiliating and physically exhausting.

Yet, amidst all the physical punishment, I began to grow stronger. Time in the weight room meant improved power and stamina. The practices I hated so much improved my conditioning, and I could work harder and longer than I ever thought possible. Suddenly I wasn't being tossed around quite so easily.

Then, one day, I won. I actually won a match. The referee lifted my arm in victory, and I was utterly exhilarated. The joy I felt in that moment made every bit of pain worth it, and the thrill of victory motivated me to persevere through those grueling practices.

Most athletes can identify with my story. Every sport involves struggle and hardship. Growth is painful, but the struggle is the very thing that breeds new strength. As the U.S. Marines say, "Pain is weakness leaving the body."

Despite suffering's ability to make us stronger, we spend much of our lives trying to avoid suffering and hardship. In fact, every tool in our garages, every appliance in our homes, was designed to reduce the amount of effort in our lives. It's a natural human tendency to seek ease, and this isn't inherently wrong. But comfort can easily become an idol, and we can mistakenly believe that suffering is the greatest evil and that pleasure is the greatest good. We can come to desire escape above all else, and this is dangerous, as desire to numb pain is at the root of many of the addictions that ensnare us.

Real men know how to suffer. They don't seek it out, but they recognize that suffering is a fact of life. They don't shrink from it or whimper and complain about it; rather, they embrace it and learn how to harness it. Brokenness is a reality we all must face. Realizing this truth and accepting it is the first step toward freedom.

Of course, suffering isn't a good in and of itself. It is a consequence of the Fall, a choice that cursed all of creation to experience disorder and decay. But only by accepting the consequences of that choice can we pass through disorder and decay to the glory on the other side. Suffering—whether it be physical, emotional, or spiritual—provides an opportunity for personal growth. It can especially help us to develop wisdom, compassion, and fortitude.

Beyond this, we Catholics realize that suffering can take on greater meaning in light of the Passion and death of Jesus Christ. Our sufferings, no matter how small, contain a potential spiritual energy that can be activated and harnessed when we unite those sufferings to those of Christ. When we choose lovingly to "offer up" our sufferings, they are in a way transformed into something new and dynamic, something that can be used for the good of ourselves and others. In this way, we participate mysteriously in the eternal sacrifice of Calvary.

The rushing waters of a river can be dangerous and even deadly. But when channeled into a turbine, they can be harnessed in order to generate enough electricity for a small town. We can choose to see the sufferings of this life as merely negative, or we can activate them and endow them with a greater power—the power to convert hearts and draw down many graces from heaven.

Moreover, suffering well can be a great witness to a world that fears pain above all else. Assisted suicide is growing in popularity for the very reason that people would rather die than endure any discomfort. Those who know how to suffer heroically and even with joy are prophetic signs to the world, signs that love is greater than any pain we encounter.

The ultimate witness of the power of suffering endured with love is the Cross. In his Passion, Christ teaches us that true love does not flee from pain or death, rather, transfigures them. As men, we must not fear the inevitable, but when the crosses of this life come our way, we must carry them with strong, heroic hearts, remembering the words of Saint Paul: "I consider that the sufferings of this present time are not worth comparing with the glory that is to be revealed to us" (Rom 8:18).

14

Courtesy

F OR YEARS, the show *Downton Abbey* captivated viewers worldwide, including my wife. There is something fascinating about the aristocratic culture of manners and propriety that the show portrays. The ornate
formality and the decorum that was expected to be ob-
served by the British upper class draw a striking con-
trast to our society, where it is not uncommon to see
someone shopping for groceries in slippers and paja-
mas.

Lord Grantham, dressed impeccably and speaking
with precision, cuts the figure of the archetypal gentleman. But must one own a multithousand-acre estate
with a gigantic stately home to be a gentleman? Must
he have a noble family pedigree that can be traced back
centuries? Or is the title of gentleman something ac-
cessible to all of us?

Being a gentleman does not require owning a large
home or bearing a noble title. Rather, one of the
quintessential attributes of a gentleman is courtesy.
Courtesy is, in fact, the hallmark of a gentleman; the
very word *court*esy reminds us that manners largely developed within the context of a royal court. As the

politics of royalty developed, noblemen grew further away from the day-to-day activities of monarchs, but their courtly manners and gentle demeanors remained.

A French expression that was once known to all upper-class gentlemen is *noblesse oblige* (nobility obliges), which simply means that one's rank and privileges obligate him to be generous, courteous, and honorable. One's rank was to be put at the service of others and used for their good. The age of nobility is largely past, but the word *gentleman* has become synonymous with *kindness*, *respect*, and *selfless service*.

A man who holds the door for the person behind him, or who offers to carry a heavy package for someone, or who, with a smile, lets another go first, or who is cheerful when he should be annoyed is unquestionably courteous. But what is courtesy? How should we define it? What is it at its heart?

Courtesy is love in little things. It is thinking of others before oneself. It shows itself in small gestures of kindness, sacrifices bestowed on others out of the sheer abundance of the heart. The courteous person recognizes the inherent dignity of everyone and thus treats others with reverence and honor, placing their needs before his own. As Cardinal Newman once put it, "It is almost a definition of a gentleman to say that he is one who never inflicts pain."[1]

Sadly, polite men who think of others before themselves are increasingly rare. Today, men are often characterized by boorish insensitivity—an elbows-out

[1] John Henry Newman, *The Idea of a University* 8, 10.

competitiveness that looks out only for self and never for others. We live in a society in which people trample one another on Black Friday to save a few dollars on a TV. It is a sign of a deeply ingrained cultural narcissism and self-absorption whose effects are toxic.

Courtesy is not optional for the man seeking to live a life of virtue and integrity. It is essential because it is nothing else but the Golden Rule in action. It is doing unto others as we would have them do unto us. Fundamentally, courtesy is an attribute of the virtue of Justice—giving to others what they are owed. And what are they owed? Respect and kindness, for they are souls made in the image and likeness of God.

But courtesy does not come naturally; it is a skill that must be cultivated. We are all naturally selfish. My four- and five-year-old boys prove that well enough! "Me" was on their lips almost from the moment they could talk. Then it became "Me first! Mine!" My wife and I must be constantly vigilant, as our boys seem to spend half the day competing to get the best of everything. Self-centeredness is a habit that must be trained out of us very early, or it will come to characterize our lives.

As fallen, broken creatures, we have a black hole of selfishness at the center of our being. Its gravitational pull encourages us to see the world through greedy eyes. And our culture encourages this mentality. Frequently, commercials tell us, "You deserve to be pampered" and other things of that sort. Advertising especially makes us dwell on our wants and needs, as if the world revolved around us.

Even when we aren't being intentionally selfish, we can often be unthinking. We become so absorbed in our own concerns, rushing here and there, that we simply don't recognize that anyone else exists. We let the door slam in someone's face because we don't stop to see if there is anyone behind us. We aren't trying to be rude, but our unmindfulness and hurry renders us so.

The only way to have courtesy is to practice it, and this takes a conscious effort. We must decide to resist the culture of "me" and begin to live a life for others. Such a life is often anything but heroic or glamorous. It can be uncomfortable. It might even earn dirty looks from those who think we are chauvinistic or old-fashioned. It will certainly rub our self-will the wrong way. But in the end, service to others always brings lasting joy, while selfishness always disappoints.

As Catholics, we must be courteous. Not in a fawning or flattering way, but in a sacrificial and selfless way. We must stop and think and realize that we are not the only person in existence. We must strive to *see* people, not as nuisances to be avoided or competitors to be conquered, but as living souls worthy of our love and respect. Only then that we will be worthy of the name gentleman.

15

The Call to Protect

THERE HAVE BEEN MANY violent shootings and attacks in recent years, at schools, places of worship, and theaters. After each episode of random violence, there is an inevitable debate over the ownership of guns. Gun ownership is a contentious issue, but wherever one stands on the issue, it should be self-evident that the right to self-defense must be preserved. For there is one thing that should compel any man to fight, however reluctantly, and that is love—love of family, love of country, love of freedom. When we love something, it is nearly impossible not to fight for it, to lay down our lives for it.

The jolly genius G. K. Chesterton would startle his contemporaries by revealing that he carried a revolver in his pocket. Why did an otherwise harmless man carry a gun? "To defend my bride," he would answer. If you know anything about Chesterton, you know he was as nonthreatening as they come. His most deadly weapon was his intellect, and it could pick off a bad philosophy at three hundred yards. But he was a gentle giant and wouldn't hurt a fly, much less a human being.

That is, unless his bride, the one he loved with all his very large heart, was threatened.

Chesterton never had to use his revolver, which is fortunate, as I doubt he would have been a very good shot. But he was ready to use it in principle, because he knew that to fail to defend is to fail to love. "Real love is not passive," Chesterton explained, "because one cannot feel it without being ready to fight for it."[1] Protection of the beloved, and of the vulnerable and the defenseless, is part and parcel of manhood. It is a special calling for us men, as God has endowed us with natural physical strength. With this strength comes responsibility to defend the weak.

My two boys are obsessed with knights and dragons and fierce combat in general. There is chivalry in their blood. The minute they see a dragon, they want to fight it. We recently bought a richly illustrated book about Saint George and the dragon, and they beg me to read it over and over. In the story, Saint George is untested in combat, but he rises to the occasion and fights to protect the kingdom—and Una, his beautiful lady. After he defeats the dragon, he marries the lady whom he defended with his life and honor. Young though they are, the boys are mesmerized by this tale of courage and chivalry.

When we aren't reading, the boys race around the house in the knight costumes their mother made. Bran-

[1] Gilbert Keith Chesterton, *Appreciations and Criticisms of the Works of Charles Dickens* (London: J.M. Dent and Sons, 1911), p. 28.

dishing wooden swords and shields, they pretend to fight off the fire-breathing fiend. "I'm a knight, Dad. I'll protect you!" they breathlessly exclaim. Combat is in their boyish hearts, and the desire to defend the good and the beautiful and to defeat the enemy is as instinctive as the desire to walk and talk.

The advocates of pacifism usually argue that we are never to fight, not even to defend others. They cite the martyrs and the sacrifice of Christ as evidence that Jesus is always displeased with violence. Their argument distorts Christ's words and the Church's teaching, however. The truth is, we can lay down our lives. We can be martyrs if we are called to be. But when it comes to the weak and the vulnerable and the defenseless, we as men have a duty to rise and to defend them. The Church has consistently taught this, and the *Catechism of the Catholic Church* makes it clear:

> Legitimate defense can be not only a right but a grave duty for one who is responsible for the lives of others. The defense of the common good requires that an unjust aggressor be rendered unable to cause harm. For this reason, those who legitimately hold authority also have the right to use arms to repel aggressors against the civil community entrusted to their responsibility.[2]

While this passage specifically refers to the civil community, it also applies to the smallest community, the family. No man worthy of the name would stand by idly while his wife and children were assaulted by an intruder if he had the power to stop him. And even if

[2] *CCC* 2265.

he were outmatched, the manly thing to do would be to go down fighting for his family. To do otherwise would be damnable cowardice, the exact opposite of masculine heroism.

Men are called to protect because, despite the claims of the more radical strains of feminism, men and women aren't physically identical. With very few exceptions, men are physically stronger than women. Even from a secular and evolutionary perspective, this fact is impossible to deny. That is why men and women still do not compete in the same sporting events, despite all the movements for leveling and equality. It simply wouldn't be fair. And because of our inherent strength, we men have a duty to defend those who are weaker, specifically women and children and the infirm.

We are called to protect because of the inherent dignity of life. Although it may seem paradoxical, it is the very value of human life that may drive us to take the life of another. Saint John Paul II explains in his encyclical letter *Evangelium vitae*:

> Certainly, the intrinsic value of life and the duty to love oneself no less than others are the basis of a true right to self-defence. The demanding commandment of love of neighbour, set forth in the Old Testament and confirmed by Jesus, itself presupposes love of oneself as the basis of comparison: "You shall love your neighbour as yourself" (Mk 12:31). Consequently, no one can renounce the right to self-defence out of lack of love for life or for self. This can only be done in

virtue of a heroic love which deepens and transfigures the love of self into a radical self-offering, according to the spirit of the Gospel Beatitudes (cf. Mt 5:38–40). The sublime example of this self-offering is the Lord Jesus himself.

Moreover, "legitimate defence can be not only a right but a grave duty for someone responsible for another's life, the common good of the family or of the State" (*CCC* 2265). Unfortunately it happens that the need to render the aggressor incapable of causing harm sometimes involves taking his life. In this case, the fatal outcome is attributable to the aggressor whose action brought it about, even though he may not be morally responsible because of a lack of the use of reason.[3]

The point is clear. We men are called to protect—women, children, the unborn, and anyone weaker than we are. It is nothing less than our duty.

[3] John Paul II, encyclical letter *Evangelium vitae* (March 25, 1995), no. 55, http://w2.vatican.va/content/john-paul-ii/en/encyclicals/documents/hf_jp-ii_enc_25031995_evangelium-vitae.html.

16

Holy Matrimony

DESPITE MY BEST EFFORTS at resistance, my wife occasionally subjects me to that cheesiest of film genres, the chick flick. We grab our popcorn and sit down to two hours of hopelessly impossible and dangerously impractical romance, fueled by only mildly amusing humor and generally weak plots.

But while these movies are steeped in the worst type of sentimentality (the heroine almost always rejects the perfectly worthy and appropriate suitor for the heart-throb who will no doubt make a terrible husband), these films often represent the reality of modern romance quite accurately. People often enter into marriage with no understanding of what it is, and they frequently choose their mates for all the wrong reasons. Chick flicks, rather than being a cause of these problems, are more of a mirror that reveals the way we think about love in a society that has lost the sense of sacramental marriage.

Divorce is the new societal norm. Almost everyone I know is either divorced or the child of divorced parents. It is not uncommon for individuals to marry and divorce and remarry multiple times, with several children from several different spouses (not to mention the children from other nonmarital relationships). This is not to point fingers or to heap blame—the causes for the degeneration of marriage are manifold—but, rather, to point out that we have forgotten what marriage means.

In the 1998 movie *You've Got Mail*, a typical chick flick, there is a scene that highlights perfectly the chaos of modern families. The main character, Joe Fox (played by Tom Hanks), tries to explain his confusing family structure to Kathleen Kelly (Meg Ryan), the heroine of the story. Though middle-aged Joe is often accompanied by two young children, they are not his. One is his aunt, and the other is his half brother. This is because his father and his grandfather, both wealthy businessmen, have remarried much younger women, and each has had a child with his new spouse. Joe is the child of his father's first marriage, so he is vastly older than his young aunt and his half brother. Humor ensues as Joe tries to explain how it all works. Finally, as Kathleen's confusion grows, a bemused Joe laughs and concludes, "We are . . . an American family."

An American family—confusing and fractured, yet making the best of it: It is funny only because it is so frequently true.

Unless called to a religious vocation, nearly all young men of the past aspired to marriage, and the sooner, the better. This aspiration drove them to mature faster, learning responsibility early and seeking education and good jobs so that they could one day support a family. But in the wake of the sexual revolution, all this changed. Sex—once reserved for a stable, permanent relationship—became cheap and easy. Men were content to wait longer and longer to get married, although marriage remained an eventual goal.

The advent of contraception meant that the main point of marriage, procreation, became increasingly less significant. The sacrifice required by rearing children was, after all, a hindrance to the comfort, wealth, and ease that exemplified the American dream. Mutual self-fulfillment of the spouses replaced the responsibility of a growing family. The central question in marriages changed from "What can I sacrifice for you, my spouse, my beloved?" to "What can my spouse give me?" And this change of emphasis revolutionized marriage.

Of course, a spouse cannot ultimately satisfy anyone. It simply isn't possible for a finite person to make anyone blissfully happy forever. The honeymoon wears off, and unless the deeper, stabler, more permanent kind of love takes root, a marriage will not last. Marriage takes work and maintenance, and there will always be moments in even the happiest marriage when a man is tempted to throw in the towel and take the easy road of walking away.

As self-fulfillment took center stage, and marriages were plagued by relational fractures, society began clamoring for easy, "no-fault" divorce, and it was granted. The rest is history, and marriage as we know it has never recovered. It has gotten to the point at which, driving through town, I see signs planted by the side of the road advertising "Cheap divorce!" Divorce is such a booming business that it is now advertised like anything else.

It's easy to point out what's wrong with marriage in the modern world. It's always a bit more difficult to articulate what is right. So, as men striving for virtue, how should we understand marriage?

According to the Church, marriage is defined as a freely entered, sacramental covenant that binds a man and a woman together for life in a mutually beneficial, procreative union. More precisely, the *Catechism of the Catholic Church* says that

> the matrimonial covenant, by which a man and a woman establish between themselves a partnership of the whole of life, is by its nature ordered toward the good of the spouses and the procreation and education of offspring; this covenant between baptized persons has been raised by Christ the Lord to the dignity of a sacrament (1601).[1]

Marriage, then, is the joining of one man and one woman in a procreative union for life. Through this loving union, love multiplies in the form of children, who are to be raised in the faith and in the fear of the Lord. When lived in its fullness, marriage is a beautiful picture of the life-giving love of the Holy Trinity— the first family.

[1] Quoting Code of Canon Law, can. 1055 §1; cf. Vatican Council II, Pastoral Constitution on the Church in the Modern World *Gaudium et spes* (December 7, 1965), no. 48.

In a world in which traditional marriage is an aberration, we have a wonderful opportunity to bear witness to the fruitful love of marriage as God intended it. It will be difficult. Many things will be working against us. Yet marriage is a sacrament of the Church, a means of grace and salvation. God will be at work in your marriage, sanctifying and strengthening you and your wife. And ultimately, your faithfulness and fruitfulness will bear witness to the unfailing love of Christ, who said, "I will never fail you nor forsake you" (Heb 13:5).

A Prayer for Your Family

Dear Lord, bless our family. Grant us the unity, peace, and mutual love that you found in your own family in the town of Nazareth.

Saint Joseph, bless the head of our family. Obtain for him the strength, the wisdom, and the prudence he needs to direct those under his care.

Mother Mary, bless the mother of our family. Help her to be pure and kind, gentle and self-sacrificing, for the more she resembles you, the better will our family be.

Lord Jesus, bless the children of our family. Help them to be obedient and devoted to their parents. Make them more and more like you. Let them grow, as you did, in wisdom and age and grace before God and man.

Holy Family of Nazareth, make our family and home more and more like yours, until we are all one family, happy and at peace in our true home with you. Amen.[2]

---

[2] *Rural Life Prayer Book* (Charlotte, N.C.: TAN Books & Publishers, 2014), p. 51.

17

The Value of Work

I AM A DREAMER. I have more plans and ideas than I can possibly execute—ideas for apostolates, books, essays, blog posts, hobbies I want to pursue, and so much more. And I dream big. I read the writings of great men who did heroic things, men who changed the world—and I want to do as they did. There is nothing wrong with this, of course. Most men have a hunger for greatness. But there is a hidden danger in dreaming so big that we miss the often silent, subtle, and just-as-heroic duty of our daily work.

When one's head is filled with grand plans, no matter how worthy, it is easy to think that the little tasks do not matter—that our work is devoid of meaning. But the witness of countless saints—such as Francis de Sales, Benedict, Josemaría Escrivá, and many more—is that heroism is often found in the mundane tasks of our employment that we would rather ignore in favor of something bigger.

The truth is, men have an instinct for wildness and adventure, for labor and striving. We were born to be providers, a challenging task for most of history. All too often, though, we find ourselves trapped in front of a computer under flickering fluorescent lights, doing tasks that seem like the opposite of creating something of lasting value. For men in such situations, producing something concrete—building a table or erecting a building or even planting crops—can seem appealing. With such occupations, one can *see* the fruits of his labor, and this satisfies the soul. But with computer work, it can seem so much more ephemeral and fruitless. What are we really *doing* all day, while squinting, tapping, and clicking for hours on end?

We are called to be co-creators with the Creator—to make rather than merely to consume. Making things is essential to our nature as creatures made in the image of a God who makes. We were made for work, for expending energy, and even in the Garden of Eden, man worked, though, of course, it was a pleasure and joy then, and not a burden.

For most of history, work was a matter of survival. If a person wanted to eat, he had to hunt or plow fields and scatter seeds. It was backbreaking and exhausting, but the one thing it wasn't was meaningless. Providing for one's family was satisfying, and it was easy to see the connection between one's labor and its fruit. But the world has changed, and while we still must work to put food on the table, for many, our work looks much different from the work of the past.

No matter what our work is, no matter how mundane it may seem, it can be sanctified and made meaningful. And what makes even the most boring task meaningful? Saint Josemaría Escrivá gives us the secret: "It is in the simplicity of your ordinary work, in the monotonous details of each day, that you have to find the secret, which is hidden from so many, of something great and new: Love."[1] In each task, there lies an opportunity, some potential that can be drawn out by love. Saint Maximilian Kolbe once said, "Only love is creative."[2] If our intention is right, to work for the glory of God, we can do anything with a greater purpose. Whether our work involves a computer or a backhoe, doing it for love makes all the difference.

Have you ever seen those "I'd rather be . . ." bumper stickers? "I'd rather be fishing." "I'd rather be flying." "I'd rather be skiing." These stickers may be harmless, but they reveal a deep discontent with ordinary life. A plague of our modern generation is an infernal restlessness, a resenting of where we find ourselves and what we are called to do. Souls are filled with what Henry David Thoreau described as a "quiet desperation".

On the other hand, I have also seen a bumper sticker that is quite good. It says, "I'd rather be right here." Heroism is all about doing what we are called to do in this moment, and doing it well and with gratitude. The more difficult and contrary to our nature it is, the more valuable it becomes when we approach it with the right attitude.

Yes, ordinary work can be hard. It can be tedious

[1] Josemaría Escrivá, *Furrow* (New York: Scepter, 1992), no. 489.
[2] Quoted by Benedict XVI, general audience (August 13, 2008), https://w2.vatican.va/content/benedict-xvi/en/audiences/2008/docu ments/hf_ben-xvi_aud_20080813.html.

and frustrating—especially when we'd rather be doing something heroic or extraordinary or fun. But it is exactly this banality that God often asks of us, and if we don't embrace it with all our hearts, we will never be entrusted with anything greater or more significant.

The report for work, the massive project, the audit, the broken tool, the bad contract: all these things are the calling of the moment. There is no point in resisting them; doing so will only make us more miserable. We must embrace them as the will of God, not grudgingly, but with humility and love.

We may be exalted in due time, and our grand plans may, in fact, be fulfilled. Then again, they may not. All things are working together for our good—this we know. But if you never do anything in life but embrace the will of God revealed in the small, hidden duty of the moment, you can still be a saint, and a very great saint.

One day, the hidden things will be made known to all. And in that moment, we will see that, if they were done for love, they were not so small or insignificant after all.

A Prayer to Saint Joseph before Work

O glorious Saint Joseph, model of all those who are devoted to labor, obtain for me the grace to work in a spirit of penance for the expiation of my many sins; to work conscientiously, putting the call of duty above my natural inclinations; to work with thankfulness and joy, considering it an honor to employ and develop by means of labor the gifts received from God; to work with order, peace, moderation, and patience, never shrinking from weariness and trials; to work, above all, with purity of intention and detachment from self, keeping unceasingly before my eyes death and the account that I must give of time lost, talents unused, good omitted, and vain complacency in success, so fatal to the work of God.

All for Jesus, all through Mary, all after thy example, O patriarch, Saint Joseph. Such shall be my watchword in life and in death. Amen.

—Pope Saint Pius X

18

Who Wants to Be a Saint?

W HO WANTS TO BE a saint anyway? Saints are boring, stuffy, and repressed, right? They live joyless lives, hands clasped around their rosaries, eyes and lips compressed in a strained look that reflects their interior misery. After church, on their way home—where they intend to scourge themselves and contemplate the torments of the damned—they bitterly hurl anathemas at a few idle heretics and sinners on the street and reluctantly toss a few coins into a beggar's cup to fulfill the duty of charity and earn merit for heaven.

Right?

Not even close. But even if you happen to see through these common misconceptions, there is still a mistaken but popular notion that only a few can become saints—that holiness is simply impossible for the common man. Saints are freaks of nature, after all, like two-headed cows—extraordinarily rare and nearly impossible to reproduce. We should no more expect to be one than to grow wings and fly. After all, most saints lived hundreds of years ago and have strange names like Saturninus of the Three Holy Wise Men. They seem distant, foreign, and remote. They represent an ideal that's impossible to live up to.

Despite their popularity, the common ideas about saints are almost entirely wrong. The notion of a bitter, repressed individual, serving a severe, authoritarian Church, ready to excommunicate the nearest sinner, is hogwash. There is no one more joyful, more human, or more fully alive than a saint.

Sainthood isn't something dry, miserable, humdrum, or safe. It isn't about becoming a pale, distant figure in a stained-glass window or a pasty plaster statue. It isn't about founding a monastery or praying eight hours a day or levitating in ecstasy—though some saints have done these things.

No, at its heart, sainthood isn't about *doing* amazing feats, but about *becoming* something extraordinary. It's about sharing in God's nature and in his divine life. It's about becoming a living model of Jesus Christ. And that's a pretty big deal. Saint Peter says something quite startling in his second epistle. At least, it should be startling if we take it seriously: "[God's] divine power has granted to us all things that pertain to life and godliness . . . that through these you may escape from the corruption that is in the world because of passion, and become partakers of the divine nature" (2 Pet 1:3–4). Did you catch that? He says it almost casually. God wants us to be partakers of the divine nature, to share in his very Trinitarian life, to be so filled with the life of God that we are radiant. That is what it means to be a saint.

Being a Christian isn't merely about following a bunch of rules or making sure we don't commit certain sins. Being a Christian, being a Catholic, is so much more interesting than that. For every no the Church gives us, there's a glorious yes. We are called to share in God's *very nature*, to share in his divine, eternal life. That is the ultimate yes—to become, in the fullest sense of the word, Godlike.

That's rather stunning. Perhaps it even sounds a bit crazy. After all, how can we share in God's nature? How can we share in his life?

Jesus is the second Person of the Holy Trinity. When he came to earth, he assumed our nature. He became a complete man, just like us in every way except for sin. Jesus united divinity to humanity and became the God-Man. This is the miracle of the Incarnation, which we recite in the creed every Sunday. "For us men and for our salvation he came down from heaven, and by the Holy Spirit was incarnate of the Virgin Mary, and became man."

God assumed our nature and became a man. We don't dwell nearly enough on this stupendous fact. But it doesn't end there. Through his life, Passion, death, and Resurrection, Jesus has opened the door for us to take on *his* nature by grace. Put simply, he became a man so that we might become God.

Being a good Catholic is about taking on God's very nature and sharing in the life of the Holy Trinity. It's about being transformed and transfigured into a glorious, supernatural creation in Christ. It's about becoming what Jesus himself is, a God-Man, while retaining our personality and individuality. Entering this state of being is to dwell in heaven; remaining outside it is to be in hell.

Although all of this might sound strange, these aren't new ideas. They're as old as the Church. The earliest Christians, the Fathers of the Church, called this sharing in the divine nature *divinization* or *theosis*. They taught that this was the calling of each and every Christian.

But how do we attain this great vocation? That's what we'll look at in the pages that follow.

19

Three Spiritual Offices

T O UNDERSTAND MANHOOD FULLY, we must look to
Jesus Christ. It is significant to remember that
when God became incarnate in human flesh, he became a biological male. This was no accident. His biological sex was not arbitrarily chosen. His masculinity
reflected something important about his divine nature.
He was a man, and he acted like one.

Christ models for us perfectly what true, full manhood looks like, and we would do well to learn from
his example. In his life, Jesus had three defining roles
or offices: prophet, priest, and king. As men, we are
called to fulfill these roles in the leadership of our
homes. Let's take a close look at each one.

Prophet

Throughout the Old Testament, God raised up men,
called prophets, whose sole mission was to tell the Jewish people the truth. Often, their message was a warn-
ing: Repent or face the consequences. At other times,
however, God used the prophets to reveal truths about

himself, to communicate his identity and his message to them, as he did with Moses on Mount Sinai. These men were fiery, teachers anointed by God.

Jesus Christ is the ultimate prophet. In fact, he is the prophetic teacher that all the other prophets foreshadowed. His mission was to reveal God the Father fully to the Jews and ultimately to the Gentile world.

Jesus describes himself as a prophetic teacher, a revealer of the truth, when he says, "All things have been delivered to me by my Father; and no one knows who the Son is except the Father, or who the Father is except the Son and any one to whom the Son chooses to reveal him" (Lk 10:22). When Pilate questions him, Christ again emphasizes his mission to reveal the truth: "For this I was born, and for this I have come into the world, to bear witness to the truth" (Jn 18:37). This prophetic role defined Christ's life and ministry, and like him, we fathers are called to announce and reveal the truth about God to our families.

When we think of education, we usually associate it with paid educators teaching from textbooks. Religious education, too, takes place in catechism class at our local parish. In other words, we believe that education is what someone else gives our children. But Scripture makes it quite clear that religious education is to take place first and foremost in the home. Likewise, the Church has always recognized parents as the primary educators of their children. The family is the domestic church, and parents have the responsibility to create an atmosphere of faith and piety that defines the Catholic home. This is summarized beautifully in the *Catechism of the Catholic Church*:

> Parents have the first responsibility for the education of their children. They bear witness to this responsibility first by *creating a home* where tenderness, forgiveness, respect, fidelity, and disinterested service are the rule. The home is well suited for *education in the virtues*. This requires an apprenticeship in self-denial, sound judgment, and self-mastery—the preconditions of all true freedom. Parents should teach their children to subordinate the "material and instinctual dimensions to interior and spiritual ones."
>
> *Education in the faith* by the parents should begin in the child's earliest years. This already happens when family members help one another to grow in faith by the witness of a Christian life in keeping with the Gospel. Family catechesis precedes, accompanies, and enriches other forms of instruction in the faith. Parents have the mission of teaching their children to pray and to discover their vocation as children of God. (2223, quoting John Paul II, encyclical letter *Centesimus annus* [May 1, 1991], nos. 36 and 2226)

The family, then, is a school of religious education. The father is the principal of this school—the chief educator and prophetic teacher of the faith. Why? As unpopular as it is to say these days, the father is the head of the home, just as Christ is the head of the Church. Fathers are entrusted by God with lawful authority and a grave responsibility to shepherd and care for their families, just as Christ shepherds and cares for the Church. With this authority as head of the home, the father has the ultimate responsibility to catechize his children in the ways of God, most of all by his example. And at the hour of his death, each father, more than anyone else, will answer before God for how well he has fulfilled this duty.

Priest

Before we can understand the priestly role of men, we must understand the high priesthood of Jesus. Like every priest, Jesus stands in the gap between God and man, offering a sacrifice to reconcile man to God and to atone for the sins of his people. What is unique about the priesthood of Christ, however, is that the sacrifice he offers is nothing other than himself. On the Cross and in the Mass, Jesus is both priest and sacrificial victim, both the offerer and the offered. No other priest can say this.

But why does Jesus need to offer himself at all? Because of sin. It takes only a cursory glance at human experience to realize that mankind has a sin problem. We're born broken and inclined toward evil, and without the grace of God, we can never do anything good. Every person knows this at some level, and a great deal of human history can be described as an effort to rid ourselves of our sins. Therefore, because of our sinful state, we need a priest to do what we cannot do— offer a sacrifice to atone for our sins. That is exactly what Jesus did for us on the Cross and continues to do at every Mass. Through the sacrificial offering of himself, Christ makes possible our reconciliation with God through the forgiveness of our sins. He provides the grace for our sanctification and salvation.

By now you may be thinking, "That is nice theology, but what exactly does it have to do with manhood or fatherhood?" The answer is that we, as fathers, are called to imitate Jesus Christ by offering prayers and sacrifices on behalf of our families. We are called to seek our families' sanctification and salvation through our loving, self-giving service—just as Jesus saves and sanctifies us through his sacrificial offering. Practically speaking, this sacrificial service of fatherhood takes three forms: prayer, sacrifice, and witness.

First, we must pray for our families, asking God to make them holy and pleasing to him. How many vocations have been born, how many saints have been made, through the prayers of holy and loving fathers? God only knows, but it is a fact that Saint John Paul II's vocation was due in large part to his waking in the middle of the night and seeing his father deep in prayer.

Second, we should offer sacrifices for the sanctification and salvation of our families. Sacrifice gives energy, weight, and power to our prayers. Saint John Paul II tells us that "prayer united to sacrifice constitutes the most powerful force in human history."[1] Skipping a meal or dessert and offering it up for our wives and kids isn't really that difficult, but it can bear lasting

[1] John Paul II, general audience (January 12, 1994), no. 5, http://w2. vatican.va/content/john-paul-ii/es/audiences/1994/documents/hf_jp-ii _au d_19940112.html.

fruit in the spiritual lives of our families. Sacrifices can even be part of our daily routine. Pitching in with the housework, playing with an attention-hungry toddler, changing a diaper, or mowing the lawn can all be sacrificial if they are done with love and a willing spirit. Family life offers us many opportunities to embrace sacrifice without our having to seek them out.

Finally, our witness is perhaps the most significant gift we can offer. How we live our Catholic faith will make a lasting impression on our children. If we're lazy about our spiritual lives, if we think football is more important than going to Mass, or if we treat others poorly, our example will teach our children that God really isn't that important. Of course, living a faithful Catholic life isn't easy, and it requires much of us. That's why the primary sacrifice we must make as fathers is to take our spiritual lives seriously, following Christ with all our hearts.

King

Of all the roles Christ fulfilled, his role as king is most likely to offend modern sensibilities. Likewise, the idea that a father, or any man, might have authority is strongly distasteful to our egalitarian values. The father has authority? The father is a king? Come on! That's outdated chauvinistic patriarchy. We've moved beyond that. This is the twenty-first century, after all. The reason for this common reaction is that we inevitably associate kingship and authority with abuse and oppression. The modern mind, steeped in demo-cratic individualism, is trained to believe that all kings must be bad, and the only noble thing to do in the face of authority is to rebel.

Yet the fact remains that Christ is repeatedly de-scribed as a king, and his Church is constantly referred to as a kingdom: "Seek first the kingdom of God" (see Mt 6:33). "The kingdom of God is in your midst" (Lk 17:21). "The kingdom of heaven is at hand" (Mk 1:15). Christ is a true king, and his Church, ruled by his vicar, is indeed a kingdom.

The father, too, possesses authority as the head of the family, participating in and picturing the headship of Christ (see Eph 5:23). This authority is not a weapon to be wielded but, rather, a mandate to serve. There are many scriptural examples of Christ's authority, but one is preeminent in illustrating it: "[Jesus] rose from supper, laid aside his garments, and tied a towel around himself. Then he poured water into a basin, and began to wash the disciples' feet, and to wipe them with the towel that was tied around him" (Jn 13:4–5).

In another Gospel, we find out that right before this scene, the disciples were once again quarreling about who was to be the greatest in the kingdom of God. The setting is the Passover; it's Christ's final hour of fellowship with his disciples before he is to be brutally murdered—and all his closest friends can do is argue about who is to be the greatest, the most powerful.

So what does Jesus do? He doesn't rebuke them; he simply shatters their notions of what authority looks like. He strips off his clothes—his royal robes, if you will—and puts on the garment of a humble servant. He begins to perform the most despised of tasks, given to the lowliest servants. He begins to wash his disciples' feet.

Men, this is Christlike authority. It is not chest-thumping domination. It is not forcing others to submit to your needs and wants. Christlike authority is the exact opposite—it is washing others' feet. It is servanthood.

Put another way, kingship, true authority, means embracing the lowliest, most thankless tasks. It means patiently teaching your children virtue through example and loving discipline. It means taking out the trash and rocking a screaming baby. It means leading by example, never asking others to do something you are not willing to do or have not done already. In short, it means laying down your life for those whom God has entrusted to your care. In the Gospel of Matthew, Jesus again drives home this point:

> You know that the rulers of the Gentiles lord it over them, and their great men exercise authority over them. It shall not be so among you; but whoever would be great among you must be your servant, and whoever would be first among you must be your slave; even as the Son of man came not to be served but to serve, and to give his life as a ransom for many (20:25–28).

As husbands and fathers, we have God-given authority. We are, in a sense, kings. But if we use that authority like a club, we will incur Christ's anger. The authority we possess is to be used in humble service in imitation of Jesus Christ. It calls us to say through our daily actions, "This is my body, given for you." We must use our authority to shepherd our families, lovingly, patiently and sacrificially.

Can you honestly say that you are the servant of your family? Are you laying down your life for your wife and children?

I think if we are honest, we will admit that we all have room for growth in these respects. Let's meditate on the words and example of Jesus in the Holy Gospel, seeking to serve and give our lives for our families. For that is true kingship.

*Fifteen Ways to Live Your Role as
Prophet, Priest, and King*

1. Pray with your children, morning and evening.
2. Bless your children.
3. Review a children's catechism together.
4. Be a student of the faith yourself. You can't teach something you don't know.
5. Receive the sacraments frequently as a family.
6. Apologize when you sin toward your family. This requires a lot of humility, but it will teach your kids the power of forgiveness.
7. Teach your children about the lives of the saints. Forget Batman and Spider-Man; the Church gives us thousands of real-life superheroes!

8. Pray frequently together. "The family that prays together, stays together."

9. Listen to your family's needs and concerns.

10. Be patient. Model God the Father's love.

11. Read an age-appropriate spiritual book with your children.

12. Be genuine. Kids have a powerful ability to detect hypocrisy.

13. Be faithful. If you tell your children you will do something, do everything in your power to make it happen. Few things are more devastating to a child than to see his father go back on his word. A father's faithfulness teaches children about God's faithfulness.

14. Suffer well. Suffering heroically is intrinsic to the Catholic faith. Teach your children to "offer it up" by doing so yourself.

15. Love your wife. Broken marriages are the norm these days, and that's why it's so important to model true, sacrificial love for your wife. Teach your kids how much Christ loves the Church by how you love your wife.

20

The Essence of Holiness

Holiness: The word is haloed by mystique. For some, it is an appealing and enthralling word, inspiring struggle toward a goal. For others, it is an intimidating word, signaling an impossibly remote and unattainable ideal. A great many men think that holiness is simply impossible for them, in their circumstances. How can I, a mechanic or a soldier, embroiled in a thousand mundane and, at times, unholy situations, be holy? The idea seems absurd.

The simple fact, though, is that holiness isn't for a select few; it is for everyone. God is not a cruel taskmaster. He doesn't ask impossible things of us. When Jesus said, "Be perfect as your heavenly Father is perfect" (Mt 5:48), he wasn't raising the bar just to watch us squirm. He calls us to perfection because he fully intends to give us the means of achieving it. Holiness is possible, and a host of saints, canonized and uncanonized, bear witness to that fact.

But what does holiness look like, especially for us laymen enmeshed in the concrete, often complex situations in the world? How can a line cook in a restaurant be holy? How can a school principal be holy? We aren't monks. We don't pray seven times a day and then retire to a cell to pray more. Our lives in the world and our responsibilities to others don't allow us often to fast rigorously or impose harsh penances on ourselves. So how can we expect to be holy, let alone saints?

We tend to overcomplicate things. I have a lot of books, many of them on the spiritual life. Often, I look at my shelves of spiritual books and think, "Are all these really necessary for being a Christian?" Of course, the answer is no. I happen to love books, and many of the ones I have are very helpful. But no one needs hundreds of books on prayer and meditation, asceticism and theology to be a saint. In fact, some of the greatest saints were uneducated and even illiterate.

The essence of holiness doesn't come down to reading lots of books, or even saying lots of prayers. It consists in one thing only: obedience to the will of God at every moment. That's it. Seek God's will and do it, and you will be holy; you will be a saint.

Saint Maximilian Kolbe, an amazing missionary and martyr of charity, put it this way: "We must pray to obtain the grace of fulfilling God's Will to perfection. Doing the Will of God is love, and love is the essence of holiness."[1]

Holiness has nothing to do with our feelings, though. Being holy doesn't mean you'll always feel great and always be bursting with joy and ecstasy. Sometimes, being obedient to God's will can be quite painful and

[1] *All for the Immaculata! Conferences of Maximilian Kolbe 1917–1937* (Libertyville, Ill.: Marytown Press, 2006), p. 72.

distasteful. Jesus himself found obedience to God's will horrifically painful. In the Garden of Gethsemane, bathed in bloody sweat, he cried out to God the Father in agony, "If it be possible, let this chalice pass from me" (Mt 26:39). If Jesus had stopped there, everything would have been lost. It is what he said next that made all the difference: "Nevertheless, not my will, but yours, be done" (Lk 22:42). That is obedience. That is the cry of the saint.

Obedience to the will of God at every moment is the essence of holiness. But although this formula sounds simple, it can be hard to carry out. How are we supposed to know what God's will is, anyway? Religious brothers and priests have superiors to tell them what to do, but for us laymen, things can be more complicated. How do we determine God's will for our lives?

There are a few principles to guide us. First, the two great commandments to love God and neighbor. When making decisions, we must always follow the law of love. Are we loving God above all else? Are we loving our neighbor as ourselves? If the answer is no, we need to reconsider our decisions.

Second, we have the commandments of the Church to guide us. It isn't popular these days to speak of obedience to the Church. We recoil at anyone telling us what to do. Yet Christ instituted his Church to guide us to heaven. The Church has spoken clearly and decisively on many issues, and, as faithful Catholic men, we should be obedient to this guidance.

Take for example, the Church's unpopular prohibition of contraception. This teaching has very practical consequences for the day-to-day lives of married men. We are faced with a choice: Our will or God's will? The way of obedience is clear, but that doesn't always mean it will be pleasant. Following this teaching in our sex-saturated modern world can often be painful. But God's will is clearly revealed through his Church, and if we want to be holy, we must deny ourselves, take up our crosses, and obey.

Third, we can find God's will in the practical situations of every day. Many times, God sends us little crosses and contradictions that can rub us the wrong way, ruin our plans, or simply be unpleasant. Yet, embracing them rather than resisting them is the way of holiness. A flat tire can be God's will. A rude person complicating our day can be God's will. A wife asking us to do chores or a child wanting us to play with him can be God's will. Even a boss's poorly thought-out orders can be God's will for us. How we respond to these contradictions of our will is the difference between holiness and mediocrity.

Finally, the advice of others can guide us. God often speaks to us through the insights and perspectives of others—whether they be spouses, mentors, spiritual directors, or trusted friends. Seeking advice is wise, but it takes a degree of humility. Men are notoriously reluctant to seek anyone's help or instruction. We prefer to do things ourselves. Yet the book of Proverbs tells us that "in an abundance of counselors there is safety" (11:14).

God does not always reveal his will directly to us in every situation. Sometimes, we simply do not know what he wants us to do. In such situations, it is our intention that counts. Do we *want* to please God? Are we striving to follow his will to the best of our knowledge and ability? If so, we cannot fail. If our heart is right, God will take care of the rest, even if it means correcting a mistake. For our part, we should move forward with peace and confidence.

If we want to be holy, we must seek to know and be obedient to the will of God. There is no other way.

Prayer of Surrender to the Will of God

O Lord, grant me to greet the coming day in peace. Help me in all things to rely upon your holy will. In every hour of the day reveal your will to me. Bless my dealings with all who surround me. Teach me to treat all that comes to me throughout the day with peace of soul, and with the firm conviction that your will governs all. In all my deeds and words guide my thoughts and feelings. In unforeseen events let me not forget that all are sent by you. Teach me to act firmly and wisely, without embittering or embarrassing others. Give me strength to bear the fatigue of this coming day with all that it will bring. Direct my will, teach me to pray, pray yourself in me. Amen.[2]

[2] Attributed to Archbishop François Fénelon.

21

The Knowledge That Matters

THERE ARE DIFFERENT KINDS of knowledge: the abstract knowledge of ideas, the concrete knowledge of facts, and the knowledge that comes from experience. Although all forms of knowledge are important, there is little doubt that the knowledge from experience penetrates us the most and even becomes part of us.

Take, for example, the learning of a martial art. One can study the different kicks, punches, and throws of the art in a book or through images. All of this knowledge can be gained from the comfort of an armchair. Yet, no matter how thoroughly these moves are mastered intellectually, this knowledge is fundamentally different from and shallower than that gained through the sweat and the pain of practice.

We would laugh at a self-professed black belt whose knowledge of karate came only from library books and who had never sparred. Such a claim of knowledge would be delusional on a grand scale. No doubt, such a "master" would be easily defeated by a student who had sparred for years.

To *know* a thing, we must put it into practice.

So it is in the spiritual life. We can have the whole *Catechism of the Catholic Church* memorized and a library of pithy quotations and maxims in our heads, but unless we practice what we know, it means nothing.

I know this from experience. I collect and read books about prayer and asceticism. I pore over them until I am positively aglow with knowledge. "What great advice," I think. "What a nugget of wisdom! This is the way to heaven!" And the more I read, the more spiritual facts fill my head. The more I fill my head with spiritual facts, the more I fancy myself a knowledgeable and devout Catholic.

But the painful question, the question I shudder to face, is this: How much do I *practice* prayer and asceticism? If I am honest, the answer is: not nearly as much as I read about them. It is easy to turn the faith into a hobby of sorts, studying it and looking for new trivia and insider information, as we would with any other hobby or interest. The knowledge of spiritual discipline then remains largely theoretical, shallow, and abstract.

This equation of knowledge with piety is like the delusion of the pretend karate master. Head knowledge profits little. The thing that matters most is faith working through love. "Be doers of the word", exhorts Saint James in his epistle, "and not hearers only, deceiving yourselves" (1:22).

Saint Francis de Sales knew that real doers are known by the way they live their lives: "So if you want to know whether a man is really wise, learned, generous or noble, see if his life is moulded by humility, modesty and submission. If so, his gifts are genuine; but if they are only surface and showy, you may be sure that in proportion to their demonstrativeness so is their unreality."[1]

The only way to avoid this deception is to practice what we know. Doing so may result in failure, missteps, discouragement, and trials. It is certainly always safer to dwell in the realm of theory. But practice, with all its risks, is the only way to be a Christian.

Due to the accusation that Catholics strive to earn their salvation, we are often quick to denounce the value of works. And while it is true that our works are nothing in and of themselves, it is a mystery of the divine economy that God *does* honor and reward our works. Our works very much matter and contribute to our salvation, for no other reason than that God wants it that way. The parable of the sheep and the goats makes this clear, for Christ separates those who did something from those who didn't. The ones who acted received the kingdom. "For I was hungry and you gave me food, I was thirsty and you gave me drink, I was a stranger and you welcomed me, I was naked and you clothed me, I was sick and you visited me, I was in prison and you came to me" (Mt 25:35–36).

I am convinced that there are many in the kingdom of God who, in this life, lacked the formal knowledge of books and catechisms but kept the commandments

[1] Francis de Sales, *Introduction to the Devout Life*, pt. 3, chap. 4, Catholic Treasury, http://www.catholictreasury.info/books/devout_life/dev 48.php.

and loved God and their neighbor. I also believe that there are many who possessed great theological knowledge and were considered spiritual masters in their lifetimes but failed to reach the kingdom because they never progressed beyond the realm of theory.

Although Catholics have a creed, Catholicism is not merely a formula to be believed. It is a way of life to be lived. It is not an intellectual castle in the clouds. The Creed is inextricably linked to the choices we make every day, to the messiness of ordinary life. The Gospels make it clear that the entrance exam to heaven will not be a theological quiz but a test of works. We will have to give an account of what we did with what we knew. "Blessed rather are those who hear the word of God and keep it!" (Lk 11:28).

22

Showing Up

B ABE RUTH IS A SPORTS LEGEND. During his twenty-two seasons in professional baseball, the "Sultan of Swat" set all kinds of records, the most famous of which is his unbelievable 714 home runs. Two of his records still stand. He is unquestionably one of the greatest baseball players of all time, not to mention one of the greatest athletes.

But before his epic success, Babe Ruth was a huge failure. He was really, really bad at baseball—record-breakingly bad. In fact, he held the world record for the most strikeouts in baseball at 1,330—a record so poor it wasn't surpassed for nearly thirty years.

So how did one of the worst baseball players in history become one of the best? Such a turnaround seems nearly impossible, but his solution was simple: He never gave up. When asked how he turned his failure into success, he replied, "I just go up there and swing. I just keep on swinging, and I keep on swinging. Every strike brings me closer to my next home run." Perseverance: that was the secret to Babe's success. "I may have faults," he was famous for saying, "but giving up ain't one of them."[1]

One of the most frustrating things in the spiritual life can be our seeming lack of progress. We pray, we go to Mass, we confess, we read books—and yet we seem to have little to show for it. It's easy to get frustrated, to put our spiritual life on the back burner, or even to quit altogether.

Here's the thing: The spiritual life is a struggle. It is not the work of a day or a moment or a single decision. Yes, God can sometimes work miracles of conversion that change a soul in an instant. But for most of us, that is not how we make progress. We grow by showing up, day after day after day. We mature by never quitting, despite frequent falls, discouragement, and darkness.

The most talented athletes, like Babe Ruth, were not born great. They put in long hours and disciplined themselves until they were exhausted. And they never stopped doing so, because they knew that, by quitting, they would lose everything they had gained. Eventually their perseverance paid off. Likewise, we become spiritual athletes through diligent practice—by showing up and putting in the hard work of spiritual discipline. And we can never quit doing so.

A wise man once said that our spiritual efforts are like so many zeros strung together. They don't add up to anything. But then, when we least expect it, God

[1] Quoted in "Babe Ruth's Secret of Success", *The Life Coach*, http://www.thelifecoach.com/762/babe-ruths-secret-success/.

adds a one in front of our countless zeros, making our pitiful efforts more valuable than we can imagine. Take confidence: Each Rosary, each Communion, each confession is bearing fruit, though it is often hidden from our eyes. By persevering in these things, we are tilling the soil of our soul so that God can plant the seeds of maturity.

In the spiritual life, there is no such thing as a waste of time. God sees our efforts and our goodwill. He loves us, and by grace he will help us reach our goal. So never tire. Never give up. Keep pressing on, no matter how fruitless your labors seem. Show up day after day after day—and eventually God will raise you up.

23

What Is a Catholic Gentleman?

W E LIVE IN A TIME where there are precious few
clear-cut images men can aspire to. Machismo
and aggression seem to be the only acceptable attributes for men of late. Still, many men pine for refinement, for civility, for a code of conduct by which
to live. And so the moniker "Catholic gentleman" is
especially striking, representing a man who knows his
duty and carries it out with a dash of style and panache.

Attractive as the image of a Catholic gentleman may
be, however, defining what it means to *be* a Catholic
gentleman is slightly more difficult. After all, the vast
majority of Catholic men today have no noble her-
itage; they do not own castles or land or have any connection whatsoever to the ruling classes from which
the title gentleman originated. So what is a Catholic
gentleman?

First and foremost, a Catholic gentleman is Catholic;
that is, he is permeated to the core by the faith handed
down for twenty centuries, witnessed to by the blood
of the martyrs, and embodied in the creeds and coun-
cils of the Catholic and apostolic Church. The faith
is the air he breathes, and his whole life is dedicated

to knowing and following Jesus Christ with his whole heart.

A Catholic gentleman is *not* the casual Christmas-and-Easter Catholic, who treats the faith like a buffet from which to cherry-pick beliefs that suit his way of life. Rather, his way of life is conformed to the truth as revealed through the Church founded by Jesus Christ. He lives by his baptismal promises, rejecting Satan and all his pomps and works. If someone pointed a gun to his head and asked him to deny his faith, he would respond like the Cristero martyrs of Mexico: "Viva Cristo Rey!" Long live Christ the King!

A Catholic gentleman does not hide his faith but, rather, lets his light shine before men and witnesses to the beauty of the truth with joy, humility, and love. Accordingly, he is a true evangelist. Above all, a Catholic gentleman loves Jesus Christ and his Blessed Mother, striving at every moment to please them, honor them, and love them with his whole heart.

Second, a Catholic gentleman is *gentle*. Gentleness is not highly valued for men in our culture. It is too often associated with a sort of milquetoast weakness that shrinks from challenges. But gentleness is not weakness—it is strength under control.

Anyone who has lifted weights in a gym knows there are show-offs who like to lift more weight than they can handle. After one or two shaky reps, they drop the dumbbells with a tremendous crash, hoping others will notice how much weight they were putting up. But the truth is, dropping weights doesn't reveal how strong you are. Anyone can drop something heavy. What is impressive is the hulk of a man who can squat eight hundred pounds and still manage to set the barbell down lightly and carefully. His gentleness reveals his strength.

Likewise, a Catholic gentleman has strength in reserve. He can defend the weak when called upon, and he can rise to face difficult challenges when he must. But he is no braggart, intent on crashing his way through life in an attempt to prove his strength. His power is channeled and harnessed, fully under the control of a disciplined will.

Finally, a Catholic gentleman is a servant leader. Throughout his ministry, Jesus constantly sought to adjust his disciples' understanding of power. Remember, the twelve apostles thought that Jesus had come as an earthly ruler, and they fully expected him to act like the king he was. Command, authority, domination, conquest: These were associated with kingship in their minds. Jesus was the promised Messiah, the King of Israel. They expected him to reign over his subjects like all earthly kings.

Even more importantly in their estimation, they expected him to share his earthly glory and authority with them, his faithful followers. More than once, they quarreled about who would be the greatest in his messianic kingdom. It is easy to call such petty striving for advancement childish, but we would likely have done the same thing. The desire for power over others is all too common to humanity.

Jesus, however, never fed his disciples' delusions of grandeur. Instead, he turned their paradigms of power upside down and inside out. When they bickered about who was most worthy of authority, Jesus exploded their views of what real power looks like. It is one of the most beautiful passages in the Gospels:

> Jesus called them to him and said, "You know that the rulers of the Gentiles lord it over them, and their great men exercise authority over them. It shall not be so among you; but whoever would be great among you must be your servant, and whoever would be first among you must be your slave; even as the Son of man came not to be served but to serve, and to give his life as a ransom for many." (Mt 20:25–28)

Finally, on the night he was betrayed, Jesus stripped off his garments—symbolic of his messianic authority—wrapped a towel around his waist, and washed his disciples' feet. In first-century Palestine, there were few jobs more humiliating, more servile, than washing someone's feet. It was a job for the least of servants. The whole idea of their rightful king doing such humiliating work was so shocking and scandalous to the disciples that Saint Peter refused at first to let Jesus wash his feet. Only when Jesus demanded it as a requirement for remaining his apostle did Peter relent.

Jesus' message is clear: True power is found not in domination but in service. Authority is found not in claiming our rights but in laying them down in order to seek the well-being of others. A true Catholic gentleman understands the power of servant leadership.

He is not obsessed with power and authority, for he knows that true leaders do not demand obedience, but, rather, inspire it by their example. A servant leader rallies others around shared values and a common vision, not merely around his personality or charisma.

Most importantly, a servant leader is far more interested in what he can contribute to the common good than in what he can get out of others. He seeks the growth, development, and flourishing of those placed under him, rather than merely their "productivity". Likewise, a Catholic gentleman asks first what he can give to others, not what he can take.

Men have not changed since Jesus' time. For the most part, people are still interested in getting as much power over others as they possibly can. It is a constant contest for dominance. In such a world, servant leadership is a radical witness to love.

As Catholic men, we are called to be Christlike servant leaders in our homes, in our workplaces, and in our parishes. In whatever circumstances we find ourselves, we should seek first the growth of those around us through service, remembering the words of Jesus. "Whoever would be great among you must be your servant."

24

Fail Forward

ONE OF THE MOST PAINFUL aspects of the spiritual life is the experience of failure. It often seems as if we fall much more than we scale the heights. All too often, our resolutions and our aspirations simply do not align with reality. Habitual sins plague us and enslave us, leading to shame, confessions that are tiresomely identical, discouragement bordering on despair, self-loathing, and worse still, doubt—a terrible, nagging doubt that maybe the sacraments don't work, that maybe we are broken beyond repair.

Exacerbating the painfulness of this cycle of failure is the fact that the world puts a premium on success, on winning. There are few labels more humiliating than "loser". No man wants to be a loser. We all want to win at whatever we put our minds to, and we secretly harbor contempt, or at the least pity, for those who fail—that is, until we fail ourselves; then self-loathing sets in.

At the root of our fear and disgust with losing is a deep-down belief that we are better and stronger than we really are. When failure says otherwise, when we are humiliated by our faults, we recoil in horror. "Surely, I am better than this," we think. And the disappointment we feel at the manifestation of our true weakness can result in anger at ourselves and at God. This is pride, and a subtle kind at that.

At an even deeper level is a misunderstanding of what a successful spiritual life looks like. We think holiness is essentially victory, a rigorous conquering of all our spiritual foes, both internal and external. We believe that the measure of success is our battles won, our feats of strength, our boundless determination. But this is simply wrongheaded and the quick road to discouragement.

A priest I know labeled Christianity a religion for losers. And indeed it is. Jesus did not come for the healthy, the competent, the strong, those who could pull themselves up by their bootstraps. He came for the broken, the weak, the sinful. He came for the losers. He came for those whom the world—and the proud religious zealots—deemed unfit, incompetent, and loathsome. He dined with publicans and sinners, much to the horror of the Pharisees and the more "sensible" folk. He healed the lame, the blind, and the lepers, people whom the healthy and the whole wished would shut up and go away.

Even Jesus' disciples were shocked at his behavior. Talking to a woman—and not just a woman, but a notorious Samaritan woman? Forgiving a woman caught in the act of adultery? Scandalous.

Christ's association with failure was offensive to the great ones of the day, especially for one who proclaimed himself to be the Messiah, the conquering deliverer of Israel. They were horrified by his association with the weak and the sinful, the losers.

But the truth is that Jesus is attracted to brokenness and weakness. He doesn't admire the strong. He is strength itself, and we can't impress him with even the greatest spiritual feats. He loves the weak, especially those who know they are weak. Those who catch his ear and move his heart are those who cry loudly, like Bartimaeus, "Son of David, have mercy on me!" and who won't stop until they are healed (Mk 10:46–52).

Jesus is God with us. He is the ineffable Divinity incarnate. This should amaze us, but even more amazing is how often Jesus went out of his way to identify and participate in our weakness and brokenness and pain. He chose to be born to poor parents who lived in a poor village. Not content with a ramshackle hut, he chose to be born amidst the refuse of animals. His entire life was characterized by suffering and rejection; he was "a man of sorrows, and acquainted with grief" (Is 53:3). And his earthly ministry ended in the seeming failure of the Cross.

Here is the beautiful truth hidden in these facts: Our Savior does not come to us in a position of strength. His entire life was an identification with, and a participation in, the brokenness of our humanity. Jesus does not rescue us from drowning by tossing us a life vest while he remains safely on the shore. He rescues us by plunging into the depths of our misery and transfiguring it from the inside out.

You have failed again? You are broken? Humble yourself. You should expect nothing less than failure. Apart from Christ, you are a failure. Embrace that fact. For until you reach the end of yourself, until you collapse in a broken heap and despair of your own efforts and strength, until you can cry out in desperation with every fiber of your being, "Lord Jesus Christ, have mercy on me", God will not rescue you.

The spiritual life is not about victory through our unaided effort. Our efforts in themselves are nothing —less than nothing. It is true that God requires that we try, that we struggle and fight, but the victory is always His. Jesus is our strength. He is our success. He fights for us and conquers death and hell on our behalf. He entered the brokenness of our humanity and rescued us from the inside out. Our victory is not found in conquering on our own but in becoming one with the Conqueror.

So give up on your expectations and aspirations. Be content to be nothing, to be a loser, though it be painful to your pride. Let Christ be your strength, your success, your victory. For God's mercy is like a stream of water. It always rushes to the lowest place.

Litany of Humility

O Jesus! meek and humble of heart, *hear me.*
From the desire of being esteemed, *deliver me, Jesus.*
From the desire of being loved . . .
From the desire of being extolled . . .
From the desire of being honored . . .
From the desire of being praised . . .
From the desire of being preferred to others . . .
From the desire of being consulted . . .
From the desire of being approved . . .
From the fear of being humiliated . . .
From the fear of being despised . . .
From the fear of suffering rebukes . . .
From the fear of being calumniated . . .
From the fear of being forgotten . . .
From the fear of being ridiculed . . .
From the fear of being wronged . . .
From the fear of being suspected . . .
That others may be loved more than I, *Jesus,*
  grant me the grace to desire it.
That others may be esteemed more than I . . .
That, in the opinion of the world, others may
  increase and I may decrease . . .
That others may be chosen and I set aside . . .
That others may be praised and I unnoticed . . .
That others may be preferred to me in everything . . .
That others may become holier than I, provided that
  I may become as holy as I should . . .[1]

---

[1] Rafael Cardinal Merry del Val, EWTN, http://www.ewtn.com/de
votionals/prayers/humility.htm.

25

No One Is Saved Alone

M<small>Y FAMILY ATTENDED BAPTIST CHURCHES</small> on and off throughout my childhood. If you have ever been to a Baptist church, especially the fundamentalist kind, you'll know that a frequent feature of its Sunday service is an altar call. Most, if not all, sermons include a "gospel" reminder: You are a sinner, Christ died for your sins, so accept him into your heart and be saved. Following the exhortation, the sermon ends with an opportunity for people to walk to the front of the church and visibly dedicate their lives to Christ. A hymn such as "Just as I Am" plays in the background softly and repeatedly, while the pastor issues heartfelt pleas to those who might be resisting the call. Finally, a few people come forward, to the great relief of the entire congregation.

An obvious trait of this style of decisional Christianity is that it is entirely individualistic. Salvation is something between an individual and Jesus: The person makes in his heart a decision to "accept" Christ, and that decision seals his eternal destiny. Likewise, once one is "saved", the entirety of the spiritual life is between him and Christ. Other than gathering

together on Sundays and maybe Wednesdays, something that is by no means essential to salvation, there
is no corporate aspect to the Christian life at all. One
is saved alone and lives the spiritual life largely alone.

In this sense, Protestantism can be very modern, for
it embraces the great modern myth that we are isolated from one another, autonomous agents who live
as if unconnected to the lives of others. The reality, of
course, is quite the opposite. We are not isolated free
agents but are connected in a great web of relationship,
whether we like it or not.

The individualistic understanding of salvation is foreign to Catholic Christianity. Catholics believe em-
phatically that we are *not* alone on our journey to
heaven but are part of a great "cloud of witnesses"
(Heb 12:1), past and present, who constitute the Mystical Body of Christ.

In the Apostles' Creed, the short summary of Catholic belief, we declare, "I believe in the communion
of saints." In the Hail Mary, we pray, "Pray for *us* sinners, now and at the hour of our death." Our prayers
are always plural, for no man is a spiritual island. We
are all connected to each other in the order of grace—
connected like the cells of a body, which receive the
life flowing from the head of the body, Jesus Christ.

Catholic life is oriented toward a corporate understanding of salvation. Baptism places us in the life of
the Church, a living community. When we are con-
firmed, we receive the Holy Spirit not for ourselves
alone but, rather, to enable us to fight on behalf of the

whole Church against the spiritual powers of darkness. We confess our sins to a priest, who is a representative of the whole Church as well as of God, for our sins are never isolated but have ripple effects on the whole Body of Christ. The priest hears our confession on behalf of the Church, and through the ministry of the Church he absolves us from our sins.

The ultimate example of our connectedness as Catholics is the reception of the Holy Eucharist. By receiving Christ physically, Body, Blood, Soul and Divinity, we literally *become* Christ. We are united to him spiritually and physically—and not to him only but also to all those throughout the world who receive him in the same manner and with the same faith. They become one with Christ just as we do, and in being united to Christ we are united to each other. By receiving the Body of Christ, we all share a flesh-and-blood connection. We are brothers and sisters in one family, members of one body, united in a mystical communion with all sharers in the life of Christ in heaven and on earth. This is what *communion* means, an intimate sharing in the life and being of one another.

Nevertheless, it is quite easy for Catholics to act as if communion weren't a reality, or as if it simply did not matter. We can practice our faith, praying and receiving the sacraments, as if we had no responsibility to one another. When we hear of Christians suffering in other parts of the world, we shrug and wonder what we can do about it. We ignore the souls in purgatory, perhaps under the impression that praying for them is outdated and trivial. We neglect to invoke the saints, perhaps thinking of them as remote and disconnected from us. In short, we seek grace selfishly, trying to get to heaven ourselves while neglecting the salvation and the good of others.

But as Christians, we are called to love one another, and love always means sharing responsibility for one another, as demanding as this can be. We are called to pray for one another and bear each other's burdens —spiritual and physical. This theme runs throughout Scripture; in fact, the Greek word for "one another" is used ninety-four times in the New Testament. Here are some examples:

> "Bear one another's burdens, and so fulfil the law of Christ" (Gal 6:2).

> "We who are strong ought to bear with the failings of the weak" (Rom 15:1).

> "This is my commandment, that you love one another as I have loved you. Greater love has no man than this, that a man lay down his life for his friends" (Jn 15:12–13).

> "If any one says, 'I love God,' and hates his brother, he is a liar; for he who does not love his brother whom he has seen, cannot love God whom he has not seen" (1 Jn 4:20).

No one is saved alone. We are saved in a community, a communion, a living body. We are all intimately connected. My merits, sacrifices, and prayers can be communicated to others, both on earth and in purgatory. Likewise, the prayers of those in heaven affect me in a real, concrete way. And your salvation, far from being a matter of indifference, should be as important to me as my own.

Christ did not come to save individuals in the strict sense. He came to call together a family of brothers and sisters intimately united to him as the branches are united to the vine. Let us, then, love one another, pray for one another, forgive one another, and bear one another's burdens, and in so doing fulfill the law of Christ.

26

Prayer

I DO NOT WRITE AS AN EXPERT on prayer, but very much as a beginner. Being a beginner, though, isn't as bad as it might seem. Being able to say, "Lord, teach me to pray" in all sincerity is a gift.

What I want to say about prayer is very straightforward. Begin to pray, and prayer will teach you how to pray. This method is deceptively simple, so deceptive that we often miss it in search of some more profound insight. But there is no other way. Pray, and praying will teach you how to pray.

The disciples came to Jesus and asked him how to pray. They knew that no one prayed like Jesus; no one else could speak to the Father with such intensity, efficacy, and intimacy. The disciples were in awe of Christ's calling the unnamable God "Abba", a term of great endearment and closeness. To them, God was distant and mighty and frightening—not a tender, loving Abba. Moreover, Christ's prayers wrought miracles. Faced with a dead man, all Jesus had to do was ask that the man be brought back to life, and he was. It was so simple, so easy. What was Christ's secret?

So they asked Jesus how to pray. Now, Jesus was

known to speak in riddles, parables, and utterances that often left his hearers more mystified than before, but not this time. His method of prayer was not esoteric or, humanly speaking, profound. "When you pray," he said, "say, 'Our Father, who art in heaven, hallowed by thy name . . .'"

They asked how to pray, and he told them to say a prayer—one of the simplest prayers imaginable, the prayer of a child. How should one pray? Simply, like a young boy asking his daddy for a drink. One must wonder if the disciples were not slightly disappointed in the mundaneness of this advice.

Of course, prayer can deepen and grow and bring us wondrously close to God. But this depth can never be learned merely from books or lectures or by following detailed methods. It starts very small and quiet. Once we strip away all pretense of being advanced and begin to talk to God directly and clearly, mindful that he is a living person, a friend, and a Father, something happens. God responds. He reaches out to our hearts and helps them to grow and expand. He draws us closer and makes us capable of deeper prayer.

All of this happens most often without our realizing it. If we realized it, it would go to our heads and we would lose everything. But because God loves us, we hardly ever realize that we are growing in prayer. We feel stagnant, and prayer is dry and dull. We know no inner warmth or light. Yet God hears and draws close, though we cannot always perceive it.

Prayer is simple, but simple is not the same as easy.

Some of the most difficult things in life are the least complex. Prayer can be hard work, for the very reason that it does not bear fruit instantly. We love quick results, instant achievements. Waiting for anything, even for God, does not come easily to modern men. Yet prayer requires patience to bear fruit. The expansion of the heart that it brings is slow and gradual. The one thing we must never do is stop praying. Perseverance mixed with patience, which some call fortitude, is necessary for genuine and fruitful prayer.

God will arrive eventually, and when he does, we will not know how we lived without him. But there is nothing we can do to make that arrival happen. God is not a genie in a bottle who answers our three rubs by granting us three wishes. He is a living person. He will respond to us when he knows we are ready and have been purified by the work of patience.

In this way, prayer can be compared to a man straining to reach an eagle soaring high above his head. No matter how much he stretches, he can never reach it. But what the eagle sees is the straining, the longing, and the desire. And he can swoop down at any time to rest on the outstretched hand.

But why bother with the effort? Is prayer worth it? Prayer is the life of the soul, the saints tell us. It is the breathing of the spiritual lungs. It is how we come to know God and grow in his likeness. Prayer is traditionally described as the raising of the mind to God. It is contact between creature and Creator. And to be in contact with God is to be in contact with life, for

God is the life of all things. When that contact is lost, the result is cold lifelessness.

We must pray if we would possess eternal life. It is not an option. Without its energy pulsing in our souls and drawing us upward, without contact with the Author of life, we die. We must pray.

How to begin? Begin by praying. Praying will teach you how to pray.

Seven Suggestions for Praying Well

1. Make time for prayer, even if it means getting up earlier.

2. During your prayer time, shut off your phone and all other distractions, and quiet your mind and your body.

3. Choose certain prayers to say every day as a matter of discipline.

4. Allow time for silent mental prayer—simple conversation with God as a friend and Father.

5. Practice meditative reading of Scripture (*lectio divina*) as often as possible.

6. Throughout the day, use spontaneous prayers, such as "Sacred Heart of Jesus, have mercy on me."

7. Never stop praying.

27

Purity

Porn addiction is an epidemic. There's no other way to put it, when forty million Americans are regular porn viewers and every second, more than twenty-eight thousand people look at porn. Here are a few more sobering statistics:

1. Twelve percent of websites are pornographic.
2. Nine out of ten boys have seen pornography before the age of eighteen.
3. The average age at which children are first exposed to porn is twelve.[1]

There's a strong chance that you, too, have seen porn in your lifetime, and maybe even struggle with it now. No one is immune, and sadly, even the number of women becoming addicted to pornography is growing rapidly. This problem isn't without consequences, either. Far from being a harmless private habit, it is an addiction that is destroying families, lives, and souls on a massive scale.

While pervasive and devastating, the porn epidemic

[1] *Pornography Statistics: 2015 Report*, Covenant Eyes, http://www.covenanteyes.com/pornstats/.

isn't all that surprising. We live in a hypersexualized culture, and if you're a man who wants to be pure, you're going to be involved in constant warfare against lust. Everything from hamburger commercials to weight-loss and toothpaste ads have some sort of sexual spin. After all, sex sells. Popular TV shows, too, are filled with graphic sex, simulated rape and incest, and full nudity, each show seeking to push the boundaries a little further than the others. We live in a world in which we must fight for purity and chastity.

If you don't struggle with pornography, thank God for this grace. But if you do struggle with porn, I want to encourage you not to lose heart. Know that God loves you more than you love yourself, and nothing you do can change that fact. Christ died for your sins, and compared with the mountain of his mercy, your sins are less than nothing. Remind yourself that you are God's beloved son and that he desires your salvation. Trust in him, repent, and begin again each day.

On the other hand, if you think porn is no big deal, I want you to realize that it is. It is a soul-destroying habit that, unchecked, will devastate your life and relationships. Accordingly, here are three big reasons to reject porn:

It hurts real women. One of the chief seductions of porn is that it feels so harmless in the moment. We rationalize by telling ourselves that we aren't really hurting anyone, and that everything we see is consensual. The problem is, this isn't true. Many women who've left the industry tell heartbreaking stories of abuse, drug addiction, coercion, trafficking, and more. The porn industry is a horrible place that destroys women and then discards them. When you look at porn, you are contributing to the misery and degradation of countless women. It changes the way you view the real women in your life too, causing you to see them as objects for your gratification rather than as living souls who are worthy of honor and respect.

It rewires your brain. Neuroscience reveals that our brains are not fixed, as previously thought, but are plastic. They can be trained and shaped by repeated actions. As psychotherapist and researcher Richard O'Connor puts it, "Neurons that fire together wire together."[2] And guess what? Repeated viewing of porn rewires your brain, and not in a good way. If you want to be an overgrown man-child with a smaller, more infantile brain, go ahead, watch porn. But if you want to be a mature man, a man who has control and can make mature choices, you need to give up porn.

It gets worse. The problem with addictions is that they are almost impossible to compartmentalize or control. Once you are an addict, the addiction always gets worse. That's just the way our brains work. So perhaps you start out looking at stuff that's relatively tame. But the next thing you know, it won't get you excited

[2] Richard O'Connor, *Undoing Perpetual Stress: The Missing Connection between Depression, Anxiety, and 21st Century Illness* (New York: Berkley Books, 2005), p. 79.

anymore. You'll need something racier and more extreme. And then you'll be looking at acts so horrible that you never could have imagined them, all because that's what you need to get aroused. Do you really want to end up like Jared, the Subway spokesman who was imprisoned for child pornography?

There's so much more that could be said, but put simply, porn ruins lives and relationships. People have lost their jobs, their spouses, and more, because of the harmful effects of pornography.

But while negative consequences are important motivators, we shouldn't stop with them. We should look deeper and reflect on why we want pornography to begin with. What drives us to it? What need are we trying to fill? Are we hungry for affirmation? For intimacy? Are we longing for human connection? Are we bored? Examining these deeper motivations will go a long way toward helping us understand why we seek out porn.

Ultimately, however, it is important to realize that purity and chastity are positive ideals. As G. K. Chesterton once put it, "Chastity does not mean abstention from sexual wrong; it means something flaming, like Joan of Arc."[3] Christianity is a positive ideal, not a negation of the body, sexuality, or anything else. Purity is about loving *in the right way*. It is recognizing and respecting that our sexuality communicates something very profound about the human person and even

[3] G. K. Chesterton, "A Piece of Chalk", *Daily News*, November 4, 1905, American Chesterton Society, https://www.chesterton.org/a-piece-of-chalk/.

about the nature of God, and then living in light of these truths. It is controlling our sexual energy instead of allowing it to control us. In our struggles with pornography, we must strive for the positive virtue of purity, rather than a mere negative abstinence. Doing so will sustain us when we feel like surrendering.

When you're trapped in a cycle of addiction, it is easy to feel hopeless. But whatever you do, don't believe the lie that you are trapped forever. It isn't true. Despair is the enemy. Reject it. By God's grace, you can be free of porn. Make a commitment to beat this sin once and for all. Focus all your energy on that goal, and use all the weapons at your disposal. Finally, entrust yourself wholly to our Lord Jesus Christ, who is able to help you. Call out to him like the blind beggar in the Gospels, "Son of David, have mercy on me!" (Lk 18:38), and never forget that he can heal you and save you.

Ways to Break Free from Pornography

Here are three powerful ways to put porn in your past.

ACCOUNTABILITY

One of the best things we can do in our struggle against porn is to be accountable. Sure, it is embarrassing to tell someone about your struggle, but it is also freeing and immensely helpful. It breaks the cycle of shame and weakens the power of addiction. In fact, I would argue that it is impossible to break free from porn unless you are accountable to someone else. One of the easiest and most powerful ways to stay accountable is to use accountability software. Knowing that someone else is going to see which sites you visit provides a lot of motivation to stay clean. There are a number of good choices, but one of the most popular is Covenant Eyes (http://covenanteyes.com). Install it or similar software on your devices if you are serious about beating porn addiction.

THE BLUE LABEL CHALLENGE

Speaking of motivation, sometimes we need a little negative reinforcement to stay motivated. That's where the Blue Label Challenge comes in. It's a simple contest between friends: You challenge a friend to stay clean from porn, and if he fails, he buys you something expensive enough to hurt. And vice versa—if you fail to stay away from porn, you must buy your friend something. For some people, the possibility of being out fifty dollars is enough motivation to stay clean. For others, maybe it's a blue label bottle of scotch that costs hundreds of dollars. The consequence doesn't even have to be financial. It could be some other kind of pain, such as running laps or doing push-ups. The point is, if you have a painful consequence hanging over your head the next time you're tempted to look at porn, you'll be less likely to look at it. It's a great reminder that porn costs—in the short term and the long term.

As I mentioned earlier, neuroscience is proving that our brains are plastic and trainable. Through repeated actions, we can teach ourselves to act in a certain way. The good news is, several groups have harnessed this new discovery to help fight porn. Purity is Possible (www.purityispossible.com) uses neuroscience, psychology, and philosophy to help you break the cycle of craving, and it's completely free. The Fortify program (www.joinfortify.com) uses techniques from neuroscience to help people quit pornography. And if you're looking for a more personal approach, one-on-one coaching services, such as Freedom Coaching (www.freedom-coaching.net), use custom training sessions to help you understand your compulsion and see others in a holy, healthy way.

28

Happiness and Holiness

W HAT IS THE ONE THING we all want above everything else? Happiness. The desire to experience
lasting happiness is universal. Almost everything we
do can be traced back to our quest for happiness—and
perhaps no one understands this better than those in
the advertising industry.

It is estimated that the average person sees five thousand advertisements a day in the forms of product labels, TV ads, Internet ads, and so on. Each of these
advertisements offers you a simple promise: Buy this
and you will be happy. Whether it is for floor cleaner
or a new smartphone, an ad features people living in an
artificial world of perfection and bliss. They are always
smiling, always satisfied, always having fun.

When we see this seeming happiness presented to
us, we desire it and the product that we are promised
will bring us that happiness. "If only I could own that
smart TV, I would be really happy," we think. And
before we realize what has happened, we have grown
restless and discontent until we can possess what we
believe will satisfy our longing for happiness.

Advertisers generally have a pretty low view of men.

Most ads targeting men prey on our desire for cheap thrills. What will make us happy? Beer by the gallon. Sex—the more partners and the fewer strings attached, the better. And pizza.

Don't get me wrong, I love pizza, beer, and sex. The problem is, these things are presented to us as if they will really satisfy us as men. And the fact is, they won't.

Why not? Our thirst for happiness is insatiable. No matter what we do, we can't seem to satisfy it. Sure, buying a thing may quench our thirst for happiness momentarily, but the pleasure quickly fades, and we are left unhappier than we were before. We go in search of the next big thing—the next one-night stand, the next car we can't afford, the next promotion at work. We want our happiness to last forever, but nothing on this earth can seem to fill the void.

In the Gospel of Luke, chapter 18, Jesus is approached by a zealous young man. Like all of us, this wealthy young man wants to be happy. And really, from a human perspective, he has every reason to be —he's rich. Even better, he's religious, having zealously kept the Jewish law from his childhood. Yet, despite his wealth and religiosity, you can sense his discontent. He has sought out Jesus because he's unhappy. He can tell something is missing.

"What do I have to do to inherit eternal life?" he asks, which is really a way of asking, "What can I do to be happy forever?" Jesus doesn't answer his question directly. He starts by giving him a quiz on the commandments, which the young man passes with flying colors. Then Jesus gets to the heart of the matter: "Sell all you have and give to the poor." The young man is aghast. Sell everything? Surely not.

It's not recorded in Scripture, but I can almost picture the young man trying to bargain with Jesus. Can I sell half of my possessions? But Jesus won't budge. He demands everything. The young man hesitates, struggling mightily within himself. Finally, he decides. He just can't do it. And he goes away sad.

When Jesus quizzes the young man on the commandments, he mentions only half of them. He doesn't mention the commandments about idolatry or loving God with all one's heart. There's a reason: If he had, the young man would have failed miserably. The young man wanted Jesus on his own terms, and Jesus knew it. Jesus demanded the one thing that he knew the young man loved more than God—his possessions.

The Gospel of Mark records this story and includes an interesting detail the other writers leave out: "Jesus looking upon him loved him" (Mk 10:21). Jesus' heart went out to this young man. He saw his zeal and his longing for happiness. He knew that he alone could satisfy this young man's heart but not until the man let go of his idols and died to himself. Christ made this demand not out of cruelty but out of love. Jesus knows that idols make us unhappy. He knows that they can never satisfy us and that, if we cling to them, we will go away sad like the young man.

The disciples are rather shocked by Jesus' exchange with the young man, and it leaves them questioning:

"What about us? We have left everything for you. What do we get in return?"

Jesus' reply is full of good news. "Truly, I say to you, there is no man who has left house or wife or brothers or parents or children, for the sake of the kingdom of God, who will not receive manifold more in this time, and in the age to come eternal life" (Lk 18:29–30). In other words, seek first the kingdom of God, and happiness will be yours.

Perhaps it isn't money you cling to; maybe it's the approval of others, or pornography, or a relationship, or comfort, or technology. Whatever it is, Jesus looks at you, and he loves you. He says to you, "I know you want to be happy, but your idols will never satisfy you. Give them up and follow me. I will bring you more happiness than you can imagine, but you have to love me above every other worldly good. You must seek me first, and you will find joy unspeakable."

If you want to be happy, seek Jesus. He is the answer to your heart's infinite longings, and he alone can bring you happiness. Reject the false promises of the world and give up the pursuit of endless things that will never satisfy you. It is a truth proven by thousands of saints that the holiest people are the happiest people. Seek Christ, and when you have found him, give yourself to him without reserve, for in return you will find joy in this life and, in the age to come, eternal life.

29

The Gift of Faith

WE LIVE IN AN AGE OF CHOICE. Name your preference, and there's something out there designed
just for you. There are clothing stores for every possible shape, size, and fashion—even stores that cater to
niche subcultures; high-end, low-end, and everything
in between.

Restaurants, too, come in infinite varieties. Drive
through any shopping district, and you will see restaurants offering different price points, flavors, and eth-
nic cuisines. Fast food, slow food, organic, vegan—
you name it.

But we have perhaps the most choices when it
comes to entertainment. Turn on the TV, and you'll
be greeted with more than a thousand cable channels.
Available online are on-demand streaming services such
as Netflix and Amazon Prime. Music streaming services are just as prevalent, and they offer a catalog of
millions of songs, often free. Anything you could possibly want to watch or listen to is only a click away.

We have so many choices that we have come to believe that we have the *right* to choose what we want.
We feel desperate when our choices are limited. How

did people survive before there were infinite options to choose from?

On a more serious level, our consumeristic, choice-oriented culture has begun to affect society in a deeper way. Women proudly chant, "My body, my choice", demanding the right to choose whether their unborn child will live or die. And now, the right-to-die movement wants to give people the choice to opt out of life altogether. Unlimited freedom and unlimited choice, unmoored from any moral boundaries, can have dangerous consequences.

We've also applied this consumeristic thinking to matters of faith. No matter how nuanced your theological viewpoint or belief system, whatever your preferred style of worship, there is a church or a denomination for you. I grew up Protestant, and it was not uncommon for people to church-shop, looking for the perfect combination of charismatic preacher, preferred musical style, alignment with personal beliefs, and warm fellowship. There are rock 'n' roll churches, cowboy churches, high churches, low churches. If you haven't found your perfect church, the thinking goes, just keep looking. There is bound to be one that is right for you.

To be Catholic means to reject the idol of consumeristic faith. Catholicism is the opposite of consumerism. It is tradition; it is submission to what has been received. "So then, brethren", says Saint Paul, "stand firm and hold to the traditions which you were taught by us, either by word of mouth or by letter" (2 Thess 1:15). To be Catholic means to stick fast to

the Creed, to receive gratefully and humbly what has
been handed down. In his epistle, Saint Jude speaks
about the faith being "once for all delivered to the
saints" (v. 3), not a faith constantly being reinvented
according to our desires.

Martyrs throughout the centuries did not shed their
blood for a theological preference or a preferred worship style. They died for the living Christ, who entrusted his teaching to twelve men, who in turn passed
it on to a multitude of disciples who followed Christ in
following them. *Martyr* means "witness", and countless Christian martyrs have given testimony to what
they have seen and heard—not their own interpreta-
tion, not their private judgment and formulation, but
what had been handed on to them. This transmission
has kept the faith intact for twenty centuries, through
wars, schisms, heresies, and divisions; it is a great river
whose source is Christ and whose waters have fed the
faithful for millennia.

Modernity, the cult of preference and of choice,
sneers at and despises tradition. It sees tradition as an
obstacle to unlimited freedom—one that must be de-
stroyed. Those who prefer having things their own
way try to erase the witness of their forefathers. "That
is the way things *used* to be," they smirk with conde-
scension, "but we know better now. We must get with
the times, after all."

But the Catholic looks with reverence upon the traditions of his fathers in faith, upon that great "cloud
of witnesses" (Heb 12:1) who have delivered a sure

testimony on the teaching of Christ. The Catholic rejects a personal religion, easy and comfortable, and, with docility born of the strength of conviction, he submits to the demands of Jesus Christ as taught by his Church.

As men seeking to follow Christ with our whole hearts, we must reject the cult of preference, of tailor-made religion. We must humbly submit to the teaching of Christ, no matter how demanding it may be, and turn again to the faith of our fathers, the holy faith handed down once and forever. Besides, embracing tradition in a world hell-bent on erasing it is the ultimate act of revolution.

30

The Marian Way

I T IS INTERESTING how kids treat their parents differently. My two young boys are a case in point. With me, they seek adventure and roughhousing. We fight dragons, have pretend monster-truck rallies, build forts, and tackle each other in epic wrestling matches. It is action nearly all the time. But the instant one of them gets hurt badly, everything changes. I can try my best to assure him that he will be all right, but he wants none of it. In such cases, only Mom will do, and he runs to find her as quickly as he can.

We've all seen images of the burly sailor or biker guy with a heart tattoo emblazoned with the word *Mom* on his arm. Toughness doesn't prevent devotion to one's mother. There is something unique about a boy's relationship with his mother. It has been said that men want to be like their fathers, but they love their mothers. No matter how rugged and hardened we may become, we always have a soft spot in our hearts for our moms.

Jesus, too, had a mother; he chose to come to us through the womb of a young virgin of Nazareth. She was poor, with no worldly honor or distinction, but she had the perfection of human beauty and holiness.

God's choice to become a frail human embryo in Mary's womb and then a helpless baby in her arms speaks of his humility. Though he was filled with omnipotence and strength, the very definition of might and power, Jesus wanted to teach us the power of dependence.

As an infant, the Son of God could not care for himself. He relied completely on another—his mother. In fact, he spent the majority of his life with his mother; approximately ten times as long as he spent with his disciples or in public ministry, preaching and teaching. According to tradition, Saint Joseph died while Christ was still young. During this phase of his life, Jesus cared for his mother, and she cared for him.

Having set this example for us, Jesus declared that unless we become like little children, we will never inherit the kingdom of heaven (Mt 18:3). How can we become like children? We can strive to develop their innocence, their wonder, their unquestioning trust, their simplicity, and most significantly, their dependence.

We like to believe that we are self-made men, dependent on no one. Yet, if we honestly and objectively analyze our situation, we will discover that we are dependent on God for absolutely everything. We do not take a breath, our heart does not beat, without his consent and power. On the most fundamental level, the ability to *be*, to exist at all, is the first mark of our dependence. Without God, we would drop into the abyss of nothingness in an instant.

Spiritual childhood is merely acknowledging this dependence and growing in trust. It is wising up to the truth that without Christ, we can do nothing. This is hard for us to do; it takes humility. But Christ knows our needs, so he went before us and gave us an example of what we are to do. That is why he chose to become a child himself. He wants us to understand what dependence means, to grow in childlike trust. He began his life with Mary and ended it with her, giving her to his whole Church and to each one of us: "Woman, behold your son. Son, behold your mother" (see Jn 19:26–27). In the same way he came to us, he wants us to come to him—through his Mother.

Remember that our destiny is heaven, our vocation is to share in the divine life, and our goal is to be formed in the likeness of Jesus Christ. There are two ways of accomplishing our vocation. Saint Francis of Assisi called them the red ladder and the white ladder. The first way is the red ladder of penance, in which we might struggle and strive with all our might, fasting, doing severe penances, praying all night, giving away all that we possess, and fleeing the world like the early monastics. The second way is the white ladder of Marian consecration. This way is easy and short, the way of Jesus Christ. We give everything to Mary, as Jesus did, and grow in our love and devotion to her, seeking to carry out her will and please her at every moment, like a child. In turn, she forms Jesus Christ in us, in our souls, in all his might and power.

Saint Louis de Montfort used a similar analogy, comparing the two ways of being formed into the image of Christ to being sculpted by a chisel or being cast in a mold. The first way is painful and painstaking, requiring many blows of the hammer and the razor-sharp chisel. It is hard and grueling and long. The second way, being cast into a mold, is quick and easy. It can be done in hardly any time at all, but it requires that we be "well molten", that is, compliant and nonresistant to the work of the Holy Spirit.

All this talk of childlikeness and dependence might be distasteful to men. We don't find the image of a child snuggling in his mother's arms to be all that appealing. The key is not to confuse the end and the means. The result of true devotion to Mary is awe-inspiring: We will become mighty warriors, made in the image of the Lion of the Tribe of Judah, Jesus Christ, who breaks his enemies with a rod of iron. We will rule and reign with him in his everlasting kingdom. We will become God-men. But the only way to achieve this high calling is to humble ourselves and become like little children first. Saint Louis de Montfort is uncompromising in his call for us to become the children of Mary: "It is through the most holy Virgin Mary that Jesus came into the world, and it is also through her that he has to reign in the world. . . . Devotion to Our Blessed Lady is necessary for salvation. . . . He who has not Mary for his Mother has not God for his Father."[1]

If we give ourselves entirely to Mary's care and protection, as Jesus did in the Incarnation, amazing things will begin to happen. She will begin to work in us and employ us as her weapons against Satan. She will put us to work where the battle is hottest. In the words of Saint Louis, that fiery prophet of Mary, "They shall be the ministers of the Lord who, like a burning fire, shall kindle the fire of Divine love everywhere. They shall be 'like sharp arrows in the hand of the powerful' Mary to pierce her enemies."[2] Give yourself to Mary, and you will be saved. Consecrate yourself entirely to her, and she will form Jesus Christ in you and fill you with the power of the Holy Spirit.

[1] Louis de Montfort, *True Devotion to Mary*, introduction, 1; 1, 1, 40 and 30.
[2] Ibid., 1, 1, 56.

31

Living Icons

W E OFTEN THINK the spiritual life comprises a multiplicity of activities: Praying, reading devotional books, going to Mass and confession, studying theology, and doing acts of penance. Although it is true that various disciplines are necessary for spiritual maturation, however, they alone do not produce spiritual growth. In his book *The Heart of Holiness*, Fr. Gary Lauenstein, C.Ss.R., described how he became embittered during his novitiate with the Redemptorists because he lost sight of the reason behind his rigorous training. His experience taught him that religion, particularly Christianity, "is not a mechanical process but a relationship. . . . It is a form of friendship—with God."[1]

Spiritual disciplines are never ends in themselves. When approached the right way, they serve to till the rocky soil of the heart, to make room for God, and to draw us close to him. They can bring us into contact with Christ so that he can change us.

Put another way, spiritual growth is not so much

[1] Gary Lauenstein, *The Heart of Holiness: Friendship with God and Others* (San Francisco: Ignatius Press, 2016), p. 11.

a matter of doing as it is of *gazing* and *becoming*. As Archbishop Fulton Sheen noted, "We become like that which we love."[2] From as soon as they were old enough to understand, my boys have wanted to be like me. "I'm just like you, Daddy," they say proudly and with beaming faces. If I put on a hat, they want to wear one. If I shave, they want to shave. If I pray, they want to pray. And if I am undisciplined, materialistic, or short-tempered, they likely will be too. They want to be like their father in every way, for children don't become what you tell them to be. They become what you are.

The desire to imitate and become like an icon does not end in childhood. Throughout our lives, we identify images that we admire and want to become. It is entirely natural, but the desire can easily be perverted or used to the advantage of others. Advertisers especially understand our desire to become something, to fit an image, and much of advertising is merely projecting images for us to desire and imitate. The more we admire, the more we desire.

Idol comes from the Latin word *idolum*, which means "image". And there is a sense in which every idol is an image that we crave to become. This can be either good or bad, depending on the model we choose. A model that is sensual, worldly, and wicked will make us sensual, worldly, and wicked. A model of holiness, goodness, beauty, and truth will transform us into its

[2] Fulton Sheen, *Life Is Worth Living* (San Francisco: Ignatius Press, 1999), p. 61

image. This transformation usually happens uncon-
sciously, without our intentional effort.

Being a follower of Jesus Christ comes down to gazing at him so intently that we become him. Saint Paul
puts it this way: "We all, with unveiled face, behold-
ing the glory of the Lord, are being changed into his
likeness from one degree of glory to another" (2 Cor
3:18). All the exercises of the spiritual life, all the disciplines, are designed to purify our spiritual vision so
that we may see Christ with an "unveiled face" and
desire him so much that we will be transformed into
his likeness.

When I was in high school, WWJD bracelets were all
the rage. The acronym for the question "What would
Jesus do?" was meant to help us make the right choices
in life. It seems simple in theory, but in practice, it's a
little more difficult. After all, what *would* Jesus do? He
lived in a very different time and place. He didn't have
to make car payments or support a wife and children
or work in a factory or fight on a battlefield. How can I
know exactly what he would do in my time and place,
in my difficulties and circumstances?

That's where the saints come in. The saints are little Christs. They lived his life after him. And the vast
variety of the saints, their different states in life, their
different struggles and sufferings and charisms, can reveal to us the life of Christ lived in a thousand places
and times.

What would Christ have done in corrupt, thirteenth-
century Italy? Saint Francis, who was transformed into

the image of Christ, shows us. What would Christ have done in the horror of a twentieth-century death camp? Saint Maximilian Kolbe, who became another Christ, shows us. How would Christ have served a licentious sixteenth-century king and maintained his integrity? Saint Thomas More shows us.

What would Christ do now, in this time and place, in your circumstances? You are called to be transformed into Christ, to live his life after him, and to reveal the answer to that question to the whole world.

32

The Cross

S AINT PETER WAS RIDING HIGH. Jesus had just asked the disciples, "Who do you say that I am?" While the rest of the disciples stumbled around in confusion, Peter hit a home run: "You are the Christ, the Son of the living God" (Mt 16:15–16). Then Jesus blessed him and entrusted him with the keys of his kingdom, giving him far more authority than Peter could imagine. Whatever he bound on earth would be bound in heaven? Oh yes, Peter was feeling fine.

But then, as they continued their journey, Jesus began talking strangely, predicting his own suffering and death at the hands of the religious leaders of the day. The disciples were worried and puzzled, but Peter was downright upset. What was Jesus saying? He couldn't mean it. He had just affirmed that he was the long-awaited Messiah, the Son of God! Surely he was only moments away from ushering in a glorious earthly kingdom—a kingdom in which, he, Peter, son of Jonah, would occupy a very prestigious position. Jesus couldn't mean it, and Peter felt he had to set him straight. "God forbid, Lord! This shall never happen to you," he blurted out.

Then something happened that shook Saint Peter to the core. Jesus, his normally quite gentle Master, turned to him with angry fire in his eyes. "Get behind me, Satan!" Jesus thundered. "You are a hindrance to me; for you are not on the side of God, but of men" (Mt 16:22–23).

Peter was stunned, humiliated, and grief-stricken. Had Jesus just called him *Satan*?

But Jesus wasn't finished. He turned to the rest of the disciples, who were still reeling from this sudden zeal on the part of their Master. "If any man would come after me, let him deny himself and take up his cross and follow me," Jesus continued passionately. "For whoever would save his life will lose it, and whoever loses his life for my sake will find it" (Mt 16:24–25).

As we read this account in Matthew's Gospel, we are compelled to ask: Why was Jesus so angry? Wasn't Saint Peter simply looking out for him?

The answer is quite simple: Jesus loved the Cross. His death was not an accident of circumstances or the outcome of a successful plot of the Pharisees; it was what he was born for. Jesus Christ came to earth for one reason only: to redeem fallen humanity—and the Cross was his chosen instrument of redemption. His whole life was like an arrow shot toward Calvary. The Cross was always before his eyes.

The disciples, on the other hand, were appalled by the idea that their Lord would be killed. They did not listen to Jesus' warnings and his calls to sacrifice everything. They were interested only in the easy, smooth road. They longed for glory and a high place in the Messiah's restored earthly kingdom. To them, their journey could end in no other way. The Cross? Far from loving it, they were horrified by it, repelled by it.

Jesus looked into their hearts and saw their empty ambition, their pride, their love of comfort, their vain envy of one another. His infernal enemy, Satan, had been cast out of heaven for the very pride and ambition his closest friends were now displaying. And it made Jesus angry. He turned to them and assured them that if they did not embrace the Cross as he did, they had no part with him. The Cross that so horrified them became the one condition of their salvation.

Far too often, Catholics are embarrassed by the Cross. The crucifix is removed from sanctuaries. The Mass, the unbloody re-presentation of the sacrifice of Calvary, is reframed as a community meal. Priests, we are told, do not offer a Victim to God the Father but, rather, preside like congenial hosts at a dinner. Homilies, instead of issuing calls to self-denial, exhort us to a mild and tolerant affability. Talk of sin and hell and God's justice is scoffed at and is replaced by a vague and cheerful universalism.

In short, many Catholics prefer the wide, smooth road. They do not see the bloody sacrifice of Christ as central to the faith—they are horrified by it, as Christ's disciples were. To these Catholics, niceness, friendliness, and tolerance are at the heart of the Catholic faith.

Jesus Christ is far from this weak-kneed, milquetoast faith, the faith that prefers comfort to all else and flees from sacrifice. He still bears in his hands and in his side the wounds that purchased our salvation. To all who would follow him, he offers the same condition: "If any man would come after me, let him deny himself and take up his cross and follow me."

As Catholic men, we must hear and heed the call of our Lord and Savior: "Repent, for the kingdom of heaven is at hand. Strive to enter the narrow gate. Take up your cross and follow me." We must reject the easy, comfortable "Catholicism" that demands nothing of us. We must not hide the crucifix but should wear it proudly as a badge of honor. Prosperity preachers, and priests, may proclaim a religion of comfort and ease, but it is the "broad way" that leads to destruction. As for us, we should say, like Saint Paul, "We preach Christ crucified, a stumbling block to Jews and folly to Gentiles, but to those who are called . . . Christ the power of God and the wisdom of God" (1 Cor 1:23–24). Let's reject complacency and embrace the Cross, for it alone is the sure way to true, lasting joy.

APPENDIX A

The Catholic Gentleman's Rule of Life

1. I will fear, honor, and love God above all others, even at the cost of my life.

2. I will honor holy things and treat them with respect.

3. I will learn to pray as if my eternal salvation depends on it—because it does.

4. I will struggle for virtue and to overcome myself, no matter how difficult the process, not sinking to the level of mediocrity and excuse making.

5. I will prefer the Beatitudes to the world's values, remembering the truth that "if any one loves the world, love for the Father is not in him" (1 Jn 2:15).

6. I will treat others, made in the image and likeness of God, with dignity and respect, especially remembering to honor and to serve the poor, the weak, and the rejected as I would Christ himself.

7. I will honor women, acknowledging their great dignity as daughters of God.

8. I will value and strive for chastity, rejecting pornography, unholy entertainment, and anything that degrades the dignity of the human person.

9. I will love the Blessed Virgin Mary in a special way and develop my devotion to her as the sure path to holiness and union with Jesus Christ.

10. I will value my body and care for it.

11. I will learn to bear suffering with patience, carrying my cross after the Lord Jesus.

12. I will carry myself with humility and integrity, taking responsibility for my actions.

13. I will always tell the truth.

APPENDIX B

The Catholic Gentleman's Reading List

There are hundreds of books I could recommend for further reading, but I will limit this list to these below in the hope that they will get you thinking and learning, pondering and praying. Never stop learning!

Masculinity

Be a Man! by Fr. Larry Richards

Behold the Man by Deacon Harold Burke Sivers

Love and Responsibility by Karol Wojtyła

He Leadeth Me by Fr. Walter Ciszek

With God in Russia by Fr. Walter Ciszek

The Shadow of His Wings by Fr. Gereon Goldmann

The Miracle of Father Kapaun by Travis Heying and Roy Wenzl

Theology and Spirituality

The Imitation of Christ by Thomas à Kempis

The Spiritual Combat by Dom Lorenzo Scupoli

Divine Intimacy by Fr. Gabriel of St. Mary Magdalene, O.C.D.

Peace of Soul by Fulton J. Sheen

Life of Christ by Fulton J. Sheen

The Secret of Mary by St. Louis de Montfort

True Devotion to Mary by St. Louis de Montfort

The Kolbe Reader by Fr. Anselm Romb

The Power of Silence by Cardinal Robert Sarah

The Way of a Pilgrim by Unknown

The Confessions by St. Augustine

Noble Beauty, Transcendent Holiness by Peter Kwasniewski

Theology for Beginners by F. J. Sheed

Philosophy

Orthodoxy by G. K. Chesterton

The Everlasting Man by G. K. Chesterton

A Guide for the Perplexed by E. F. Schumacher

In Tune with the World by Josef Pieper

Leisure: The Basis of Culture by Josef Pieper

The Restoration of Christian Culture by John Senior

A Mind at Peace by Christopher Blum and Joshua Hochschild

12 Rules for Life by Jordan Peterson

Marriage and Family

Christ in the Home by Fr. Raoul Plus, S.J.

Three to Get Married by Fulton J. Sheen

The Head of the Family by Clayton Barbeau

The Theology of the Body for Beginners by Christopher West

Ten Ways to Destroy the Imagination of Your Child by Anthony Esolen

Men, Women, and the Mystery of Love by Edward Sri

Miscellaneous

The Art of the Commonplace by Wendell Berry

The Gentle Traditionalist by Roger Buck

Cor Jesu Sacratissimum by Roger Buck

The Lord of the Rings by J. R. R. Tolkien

The Seven Storey Mountain by Thomas Merton

Drinking with the Saints by Michael P. Foley

The Beer Option by R. Jared Staudt